Walking the Way

A Story of Strength, Courage, and My Introduction to Spirit

Mediumship by Picasso Publishing
Mediumshipbypicasso.com

Laura "Picasso" Roberts

Walking the Way

A story of strength, courage, and my introduction to spirit

Mediumship by Picasso Publishing
135 Jenkins Street
Suite 105B #206
Saint Augustine, FL 32086

MediumshipbyPicasso.com
facbook.com/mediumshipbypicasso
Email: picassoroberts53@gmail.com

First Published 2020

Copyright text @ 2020 Mediumship by Picasso

Cover Art by Reina Cottier Art Copyright 2002 Mediumship by Picasso LLC

All Rights Reserved

Library of Congress Control Number: 2020916356

ISBN: 978-1-7353328-0-2
E-book ISBN: 978-1-7353328-1-9

All rights received. No part of this publication may be reproduced, scanned or disturbed in any printed or electronic form, whole or in part, without written permission of the copyright holder..

Printed in the United States of America

For the record!

"All know the way few actually walk it"
Bodhidharma

Fate whispers to the warrior, "You cannot withstand the storm" and the warrior whispers back, "I am the storm."
-Unknown

OUR DEEPEST FEAR

Our deepest fear is not that we are inadequate. Our deepest fear is that we are powerful beyond measure. It is our light, not our darkness that most frightens us. We ask ourselves, Who am I to be brilliant, gorgeous, talented, and fabulous? Actually, who are you not to be? You are a child of God. Your playing small does not serve the world. There is nothing enlightened about shrinking so that other people will not feel insecure around you. We are all meant to shine, as children do. We were born to manifest the glory of God that is within us. It is not just in some of us; it is in everyone and as we let our own light shine, we unconsciously give others permission to do the same. As we are liberated from our own fear, our presence automatically liberates others. – Marianne Williamson

Table of Contents

What is Walking the Way?...viii
Introduction ……………………………………………………..xii

Chapter 1 1
Side Step….At the Heart of Good and Evil 12
Chapter 2 19
Chapter 3 26
Side Step….Smiling Eyes 35
Side Step….The Arrangement 41
Chapter 4 45
Side Step….Unbreakable 48
Chapter 5 53
Side Step….Brotherly Love...53
Chapter 6 76
Side Step.... Endometriosis: My Journey................................78
Chapter 7 102
Chapter 8 127
Side Step….Fontana di Trevi 128
Chapter 9 145
Side Step….The Transition 146

Side Step….Band of Gold	155
Side Step….Green Water	160
Chapter 10	169
Side Step….Glass Bubbles	180
Chapter 11	193
Side Step….A Primitive Place	203
Side Step….Begin Again	211
Side Step….I Belong	217
Chapter 12	219
Side Step….Dear Mom…	223
Side Step….9 Stamps	230
Chapter 13	237
Side Step….Rainbows and Roses	237
Side Step...It's All About The Energy	261
Chapter 14	265
Side Step….Strange Love	271
Side Step….The Many Faces of Death	278
Chapter 15	283
Acknowledgements	306

My 15 year old self

What is the Walking the Way?

Walking the way can mean many things to many different people. For me walking the way is a journey of healing, survival and self discovery. It is also about the growth of my soul as I am here in this human experience. It's not only self discovery but the discovery of what it means to walk the way in and out of life lessons. Through the gut wrenching times of illness, pain, grief, and loss or heart ache. It's walking the way through the good, the bad and the ugly, to finally see the light on the path and then be that light for others.

Walking the way can also be defined as simply following your gut instincts, or intuition. Thinking back on all that you have been through, what would life have turned out to be had you listened to your intuition the first time?

Walking the way is also about discovering your purpose. Usually this is found after many hearty hikes through sludge and bullshit. Tune in and listen. It is about taking part in your own existence. It's up to you. Are you going to let the fears and frustrations of others pull you into that arena or are you going to walk on to something that feels better?

In my experience I have known only to walk through the pain and suffering to survive. What I have learned now is the letting go part. It's taken me decades and it is still not perfected, but I am only just me. Not perfect but still learning my way.

Walking the way is not a thing, it is a way of being. It is the soul's growth. Using courage, strength, faith and finally love of the self.

Walking the way is about finding the light so that you can help rid others of the darkness that dwells within.

Trust me I have, myself, been pulled into illness and pain that I have manifested on my own. Instead of immediately acknowledging the choice I had, I hung on to the pain. It is what I thought I had to do. I have now learned to feel it, walk my way through it and let it go as I walk away from it. Like holding sand in your hands. You know what it is, you can feel it now, and watch it slip through your fingers delicately or not so delicately.

Walking the way is moving through life rather than standing still. It is being the river rather than the boulder in the river.

How do you know where to go, where to turn? And what to do when you get there. Keep moving and stand in faith that the river will carry you on to that next thing you are meant to experience.

As you walk into and eventually through these experiences you become lighter and more joyful. It may be scary and lonely at times, but keep moving and your path will reveal itself.

I am a warrior soul so my tendency is to battle, especially when it comes to helping the underdog. Walking the way out of a battle is mystical and fascinating. When I take a closer look it becomes clear as to why I am here. I am here to give back. I am here to show others how to survive and to have faith and courage.

Soothing the soul as you move through life comes from faith.

Stand in faith and know that things will be better. Have hope and things will be better. Let go of things that don't serve a purpose for you and things will be brilliant. Walk the way into your strength, courage and faith and you will rise to find your purpose in this life. This is where you will shine the light of a thousand stars. Bringing to you a light that can never be diminished.

Introduction

You don't know me, but I guarantee that you know someone just like me. Look around, wherever you are, and there are women and men just like me. Wounded and healed, or healing. The wounded are fighting to survive, and surviving.

I am in a constant state of shock that I am still alive at the age of 54. I look around every birthday and say, well shit, I actually made another year complete. Who knew I would last this long?

I always wanted to document how things came to be in my life, but never thought I would actually sit down and do it.

Jennifer King, my best friend, encouraged me to start a blog. She said, "Just start writing."

So I did.

I started a blog called This Seeker's Journey while I was stuck in the jungle in Panama, Central America. I had no idea what I was doing, but I was putting words to paper.

In that jungle, with my shitty computer that was held together by Scotch tape, a wine rack, and an external keyboard, words came out and I grew as I wrote. You will read some of that in these pages in sections I'm calling "Side Step".

I did that because it was, in those moments, that I felt the pain and the need to walk back through it.

I walked the way through trauma and abuse, and I also walked the way to joy and peace.

I know; I know. Everybody has a story. Mine is no different, except that it is mine.

I am sharing these experiences in hopes that you will find the courage to do the same. When we shine light onto our darkness, that darkness has no power. It has to heal.

This is what happened to me.

Here's how.

Chapter 1

It's morning. The dank hotel room is finally quiet except for the sound of my faint sobbing.

I am hidden from the rest of the world, my face pressed against the glass patio door. Condensation slowly drips past, but can't keep up with the tears rolling down my raw cheeks.

It feels like the world has stopped and there is no blood pumping through my veins.

I am colder than cold.

I am dead inside.

On the floor, I am tucked between a thick, musty curtain and cold glass. I am hiding. Willing myself to be as small as humanly possible. Isn't that how we do it? If we make ourselves small enough we become invisible. At this point I would give anything to be invisible.

My parents' drunken blow-out the night before would be the last one I would take. Here was my line. My boundary. Enough was enough.

There would be no more nights of calling the police. No more getting pulled out of bed to hide my mother. No more screaming and pounding on doors, only to wake up the next morning and pretend nothing had happened.

I would no longer mix her cocktails and empty her ashtrays. He would no longer tower over me, shouting his pain at me, that was meant for my mother.

What the fuck would I do now? What could I do? Where was there a place for me?

Crouched and crying in my cousin's room at the hotel-turned-time-share managed by her parents, my aunt and uncle. This was her space, not mine.

I didn't have a space. That was the problem. I didn't fit in. I didn't belong. Same old, same old.

There wasn't room for me here, in this South Lake Tahoe dump my family had moved to. The tiny two bedroom apartment with a minuscule bathroom the size of a small closet and a white trash family of six crammed on top of each other. My place was on the couch. There was no bed, dresser or closet for me to keep my few worldly possessions: a small box of childhood belongings and two paper sacks of clothes.

Add alcohol and drugs to this scene and you have a tasty recipe for the ultimate fist-flying family of destruction.

Home sweet home. Not any more.

At that time, my mom was on her second of three husbands and it wasn't going so well. There were only slight improvements being made with each marriage. The one thing each husband had in common was, they were all three extremely volatile in one way or another.

Just to clarify, Lloyd was her first husband. I called him dad. He was my father by name only. Then there was her second husband, my stepdad. I called him Bob. She divorced Bob and remarried much later to her third husband, Tom. He was my second stepdad. Before she divorced Lloyd my mom had an affair with a man by the name of Leonard. He is my biological father. Is your head spinning? Now imagine yourself as a kid trying to keep it straight.

I was one of six kids, and the spitting image of my mom, Geneva Laverne. This didn't bode well for me when my stepdad was drunk… which was more often than not.

He freely took his anger out on me. It was like hitting his wife without actually making physical contact. This was sweet revenge for him. He played out all of his rage and pain without his wife even realizing it. Transference… table for one?

The line up of the family went like this:

Bill, the oldest, and self made career criminal, dropped out of school years earlier to work on his passion of taking drugs and stealing from whomever or whatever. It was all about what he wanted and nothing else. In his younger years, he spent time at a boys ranch. Later, the swinging door of the local juvenile hall (or, as it is affectionately known to those who visit often, "juvy") served as his getaway.

The second oldest was my step-sister, Barbara. She was already out of school and living with her boyfriend by the time the family moved to the microscopic two-bedroom hell hole in South Lake Tahoe.

Gary was the third oldest. He was not that interested in finishing school, living instead with friends in the home town he would never escape from. He was, however, interested in drinking himself into oblivion. Alcohol fueled his rage. As I had plenty of first-hand experience with this rage, I knew I would never be able to connect with him.

This leaves the two younger brothers.

Robert, just a few years younger than me, stayed out of the house as much as he could. As it turns out a well-known "gentleman" down the road (who was not so gentlemanly) took Robert under his wing. Nobody knows if his intentions were of integrity or not. At the time nobody questioned a thing.

Last came the baby of the family, Danny. I babysat Danny more than any of the other kids. He was the youngest of us all. Because of where he landed in the line up he learned to manipulate our drunken parents to get what he wanted. He was a master at the craft of manipulation by the age of six.

I fell exactly in the middle. Two older brothers, two younger brothers, and an older step sister. I was fourteen years old when my world came crashing down. Much later in life I would realize it was the greatest gift my mother ever gave me. At the time, it felt like I had been broken beyond repair.

My family had just moved from a small college town, Chico California to the gambling tourist town of South Lake Tahoe, without me. It was my ninth grade year, and I begged for them to leave me so I could graduate with my class. What would they care about leaving me behind? As it turned out it would make it easier on them if I wasn't there. The family moved, and I stayed with my mother's mother, Gramma Bea.

Sweet, naive, baseball-watching, biscuit-making Gramma Bea. She didn't cuss, drink or smoke. She did have nine children of her own, and it was her belief that she was put on this earth only to bear children. That's it.

She had a passion for gardening, crossword puzzles, sports and raising babies. Truth be told, it would be her oldest girls that raised the babies Beatrice kept popping out.

There wasn't enough money to keep having children back then, but that's what she knew, so that's what she did. Welfare would take care of what her letch of a husband would not.

It wasn't her fault she married a pervert. She stayed, though, and for that, she is culpable. That, and the fact that she served up her daughters to her pedophile husband, and they, in turn, did the same with their daughters. And so on.

Change was the only thing I could count on. The last straw coincided with my arrival in South Lake Tahoe.

Going back to that "morning after…"

I quietly uncurled myself from the hiding hole I shrunk into and replayed in my head memory of the night before.

Unbeknownst to me, while I was hanging out at the pizza place where my cousin worked, my mom and aunt and uncle had started drinking at my aunt's house. It was late in the afternoon when I went home to find no one there. So, I walked over to my aunt's to see what shit storm was brewing.

I started to get that feeling -- you know the one -- where the wheels start to get a little wobbly but you can't do anything to avoid going off the rails.

When the alcohol fueled courage surfaced in my mom, she, in her infinite wisdom, convinced me that it was my job to retrieve going-out stuff from home so she could go out dancing (without her husband, of course). You know, make up and high heels and a slutty dress. I would do anything for my mom as long as I had knowledge of her whereabouts. It was my job to know where she was and what she was up to, especially when she was drunk. So, like a warrior going into battle I marched myself home to put things together for her. As I put her make-up and clothes in a bag, my step dad showed up.

He ripped her things from my hands and screamed, inches from my face, to get the fuck out of his house and "if your mother wanted her shit she could come home and get it herself."

I abandoned my mission, crying and seething inside. My step dad was teaching me the true meaning of hate. When I stood up to my mom and declared in front of God and everyone that her husband was an asshole, her shame and anger brought out her horns.

Drunk and delusional, she screamed at me, "Stay the fuck out of my house." I don't ever want to see your face in my home again".

I fucked up. I had revealed too much. People began to see the inside story, the truth.

It was official. I was done, and I had nowhere to go.

All I was doing was protecting her drunk ass. In that hotel room the next day, my cousin tried to convince me there was a miscommunication. Maybe I misunderstood what "get the fuck out of my house" meant.

Dee Dee suggested I call my mom and feel out the attitude. Had she really meant what she said?

I thought, "Seriously, you want me to throw salt on my open wound?" But I trusted and looked up to Dee Dee, so, I figured maybe she was right.

Already feeling unwanted and outcast, I had to reach out for a life line and hope for the best. It was my mom, after all. I had protected her so many times before, she owed me this one. Moms have to love their kids, right?

Experience reminded me what I knew to be true. That started the tears as I dialed home.

When I heard the breath of my mother on the phone I asked her, "Did you mean what you said last night?" Geneva Laverne roared through the telephone line, "Don't be such a stupid child," followed by a tirade of threats of suicide and other fun-filled antics.

I hung up and went to retrieve all of my worldly possessions: a box of childhood belongings(a ballerina picture, some pen pal letters, a cherished angel Christmas ornament given to me by my grandma) and two paper sacks of clothing. When I walked into that dump, the air was dense and filled with stale cigarettes, unfinished rum and Cokes and a thick veil of acrimony. I waded through the sludge and recoiled at the poison spewing from my mother's mouth.

I kept moving. Tears streaming down my already swollen face, I grabbed my stuff and walked out the door of the hole that we called home.

I didn't look back.

I stayed with my cousin in that hotel room and worked hard to get the money together for an apartment. I called on my mom's first husband, Lloyd, for a loan. I didn't expect the help, but he surprised me with a loan for a few hundred, which was enough money for half of the first month's rent on an apartment I shared with my cousin.

I lied about my age and managed to get three jobs in a very short period of time. Each one grittier and greasier than the next.

I learned one very important thing about survival early on: a job in the food industry means you will never go hungry.

It was summer of 1980. Every day, I lived in fear of not surviving. All the while, I kept up the charade I'd created to keep my jobs, knowing my house of cards could come tumbling down at any given moment.

Two good things about living in the tourist town of South Lake Tahoe, were that there will always be jobs, and it's easy to blend in. I did my best, but since I knew I was only fourteen, I could never let go of the feeling I didn't belong. I had to fake it if I was going to make it.

The whole dramatic mess of leaving home went down during summer break. I hadn't even thought about being able to continue my education in the fall. College had always been a dream of mine, but that wouldn't happen if I couldn't finish high school.

My dreams were rapidly slipping away from my fourteen year old self.

My family is a dysfunctional assortment of drunks, liars, cheats, and thieves. Throw a few bastard children into the mix of a "his, her's and their's" dynamic, and you get a combination of The Brady Bunch (only because of the blended family), meets The Waltons (only because they mostly lived in the country and were poor), meets The Jerry Springer Show (because they are all batshit crazy).

I mean, seriously. I made my first rum and Coke and learned the importance of keeping the ashtrays empty for guests by the time I was eight years old. A true hostess in the making, thanks to Mom.

Side Step....At the Heart of Good and Evil

My Grandfather lay on top of me, his leathery, wrinkled hands swept under my legs to get me into position.

He stayed there for what seemed like an eternity.

He looked into my twelve year old eyes and said, "Now see, doesn't that just get you shook up inside?"

What could I say?

We were in the front seat of my grandpa's pickup truck and hidden by giant old oak trees and rolling hills. The stillness of the remote countryside was haunting. I heard the crackling of the now cooling engine, the loud drone of cicada bugs in the distance, and the mouthy rasp of his breath in my face. He had just assumed the position of raping his daughter's daughter.

He didn't do it. He simply assumed the position.

We were both fully clothed. I felt confused and I felt dirty, and didn't I know why he was doing this.

He said he was preparing me for what would come. For what the boys would try to do to me. It was a ruse. A deception.

What he did scared me, but I was even more bewildered by why I would need to know what he was trying to show me. I liked boys, but hadn't even had my first kiss.

I had always wanted to spend time with Grandpa, like the older kids. He had no time for the younger kids. Well, younger than twelve, anyway.

That visit is burned in my memory. It started as strangely as it finished.

He Picked me up at my house in Chico. It was just grandpa and me for a few hours in the car as we drove to his house in San Andreas. This is a part of California that is sparsely populated. It's too dry to farm anything and has too many earthquakes for most people's liking.

For what seemed like the whole drive, he talked about penises. He kept reiterating that no matter what anyone tells you, all men have the same size penis.

It probably wasn't the entire trip, but to my pre-teen ears, it might as well have been.

I had wanted to go to Grandpa's house to ride horses and hike and fish. That's what any kid wants, right? Well, we did all of that, but he also wanted other things.

Most mornings he would sneak up behind me and wrap his arms around my body, touching my tiny breasts as much as he could while still making it seem accidental. He smelled like horses, cigarettes, and nasty old man.

At this point he wasn't even married to my mom's mom. He was with his third wife, Mary.

She paid no attention to me, or to what was happening.

He waited until Mary left to go to the market. Then he would say, "Let's wrestle. What? This old man wanted to wrestle with his granddaughter? It didn't make sense at the time. It felt more like predator and prey.

He kept trying to grab me and pin me down. Having wrestled with my brothers, I could hold my own, and ironically, I was afraid of hurting him.

I did just that. The old man's skin was much thinner than expected, and he began to bleed. That stopped him. How would he explain to his wife that he bruised to the point of bleeding wrestling with his twelve year old granddaughter?

I was beyond confused. Did he love me like he loved his daughter, or did he hate me enough to abuse me? I think it was both.

Had it not been for me getting my period on that visit, I fear much worse would have happened. As I learned later in life, it had happened to others before me.

In my memory, my grandpa was always dressed in black: black cowboy hat, black cowboy boots, and shiny silver buckle. His face was weathered and wrinkled, and his eyes -- the bluest of blue -- were always glazed over. He always showed up to our house in the middle of the night, usually drunk.

Although he was a pedophile, I choose to keep other memories besides that of him laying on top of me, pressing his old body into mine. I can't help but remember him letting me drive that old truck, and shooting the shotgun. We went hunting for jack rabbits, fishing for bass, and horseback riding. Those are the memories that help me balance the old man into what I wanted him to be for me.

He didn't know how much I just wanted him to be my grandpa.

The odd finish to this visit was he never drove me home. He put me in a car with a stranger. It was his daughter's (from another marriage) boyfriend, who happened to be going that way.

That is where my search ended. I knew there would never be a grandpa to love me for the granddaughter I was.

Did I ever tell anyone? No, because I am the one who begged to go. That's how a child's mind processes it.

Karma played out. My grandpa eventually passed away from prostate cancer.

Imagine that.

By the time I was fourteen years old, my family moved twelve times. Just sitting here thinking about it, I have to shake my head. Who does this?

Eviction after eviction made us professional movers by my sixth grade year. My parents would toss a box in the room and say, "Pack it up." Looking back I forget who was responsible for the infamous socks box in our moves. You know the one where all the socks were thrown into a box because nobody wanted to fold them. Please tell me we weren't the only ones who had a socks box? I think the socks may have gone by the way side each move. If you didn't claim them they may not have survived the move. Damn that socks box, what a pain in the ass. Maybe that's why I don't like to wear shoes and

1967

socks to this day. It's just easier being barefoot. Sure, that'll be my story as to why I hate to wear shoes and why now my feet are wide as a mother in laws ass.

Unfortunately, the moves were part of our existence. It played hell on keeping friendships, and it was worse when it came to keeping school straight. There was no explanation we could give our friends as to why we had to leave again. It was a shit show, and the adults were absolute thoughtless assholes, who were definitely not adulting.

Chapter 2

I was working three jobs the summer of 1980. When school began, I could only work nights. That sometimes meant closing the restaurants at one or two in the morning to get as many hours as I could. I soon found out that falling asleep in Algebra was unacceptable to my teachers, and anyway the pace was killing me.

Getting only four hours of sleep between work and getting up to catch the school bus could only last for so long. This had to end. I had to make a plan.

The last thing I wanted to do was call Lloyd, my father by name only and mother's first husband. I hadn't paid him back the money I borrowed. I knew he didn't want me there. He wasn't really my father. Everyone knew it.

A big fat family secret, given to me at 8 years old. I cherished that secret because it made me feel closer to my mom. It made me feel special. Here is how I found out the truth of who my real dad was.

One morning while living in a beautiful canyon house (the site of a future eviction) miles out in the country, my mom decided to keep me home from school one day.

Mom had a plan. She said, "Let's ride our bikes to town; it'll be fun; just us girls."

Even at the age of eight, I knew it wasn't a good idea, but it was a plan nonetheless. It was a few miles' walk out of the canyon to get to the main road. There were two bicycles.

The thing is, my mom didn't know how to ride a bike very well, and I couldn't teach her. She would get on, and then fall off. It would have been hysterical if it wasn't so sad. This was a disaster waiting to happen.

So we walked the few miles out to the main road, where at least it was smooth. Once able to ride on a smooth surface, we could make some headway.

Still, my mom kept falling off, and I couldn't figure out why. Maybe because she was so top-heavy. I mean, listen, mom could have easily put Dolly Parton to shame in a big boob contest.

I kept prompting her, "Come on Mom, you can do it. Just keep your feet peddling". We were so far out in the country it seemed hours before we actually saw a house, or a car driving by. By then, mom had given up and made the executive decision that we would walk the bikes.

It was even farther along the road when she bent down and said, "We are going to a friend's house, and you can't tell anyone. Got it?"

Yeah, I had it, all right. More secrets, and this time it involved more than just the two of us.

Eventually we walked up to a small white cottage. This house was so small and dark inside, I was afraid to make a move right or left, up or down.

I remember when my mother knocked there was a nice man that let us in. We sat down and must have looked a mess: hot, sweaty and out of sorts. The man smiled with his eyes first, and then with his rugged but gentle face. His eyes twinkled with a kindness that I had never seen before.

He said, "Hey, little girl. Want a coke?"

I didn't say anything, just nodded shyly. I sipped my coke and listened to their conversation, all the while trying not to burp the fizzy sweetness too loudly. Eventually, I couldn't help but let out a whopper of a burp, but the man only smiled and laughed -- not at me, but with me.

I liked this man.

He leaned over and said, "Hey, I found something the other day and thought you might like it."

He pulled a little ruby and diamond ring out of his pocket. It was small and beat up, but pretty.

Nobody had ever given me something so grown up.

I accepted the ring with a thank you. He patted me on the head and it felt like angel wings had given me the respite I needed to get through that next part of my journey.

My mom had called the step-dad to meet us around the corner for a ride back home when he got off work.

She had a plan that day, and she made it work. It took lies, deception and the strength of my eight year old legs, but it all came together.

It was a few months later -- after we had moved again -- that I curled up with my mom on a dark "hangover" day and was told that the man I met that day was my real father; my father by blood. A father I liked and wanted to know.

As it turned out, I would never be allowed to know him and love him like a daughter should love her father. This "truth" that she shared with me would have to be kept a secret.

"Nobody is ever to know, ever," she said. "If you see him on the street, don't say anything. You can't tell a soul."

"OK, Mom," I said. "Got it".

That secret that kept me from belonging to anything or anyone, ever. It created a connection to my mom that nobody could ever take away.

This wound would seep from my soul for the rest of my life. Or so it seemed.

This situation already stank of regret and failure and I had only just arrived at "dad's" house. It was one thing to be forced to take care of his kids once every other weekend, but it was a completely different thing to take on a teenage girl in the throes of an emotional and physical war. Especially when I wasn't even his daughter.

He must have been drunk when he said yes to me.

I walked around shell-shocked and not sure what to do next. I felt raw and ready to strike out. I would hurt them before they could hurt me again.

Lloyd and I had both been through the wringer but neither of us had the tools to get to a healthy place. There would be no rhythm found in this home. No music, no love, no beat or forward motion to keep me going.

Lloyd started drinking at noon or before everyday. This was and would always be his normal. It became my responsibility to secure a ride to school. It was too far to walk, even for me.

With Lloyd being too drunk to drive most days, I would need a bike. That meant I needed money, and because options were not being offered to me I figured it was time to set about getting a job.

It took all of a few months before my staying out late with friends, paired with my smart mouth, got me the boot from his home.

It didn't bother him that roaches were crawling over my arms as I sat on his couch, or as laid in my bed. That part was ok.

He had a problem with me looking like his first wife. Drinking and slurring his words was ok but me escaping into the night with friends was not going to work for him.

I had turned fifteen by this time and I had been tossed out again. Kicked to the curb by yet another upstanding citizen of the alcoholic scourge that would make up my family. I soon learned to stop asking why.

My Biological Father Leonard Barnes

Chapter 3

My wounds were becoming deep layers of pain that would take years to recover from. In the meantime, I would have to get wise.

While couch surfing at my friend Shelda's house I found out about a school program called Youth Conservation Corps. YCC could help keep me afloat for a few months anyway, and help me not starve to death. I would technically still be in school and getting credits. There is a part of me that never wanted to give up on my education. Working with YCC kept me connected to school.

The only problem with this program was it was usually filled with rich kids with good grades and full bellies. I had a high GPA in junior high school; maybe they would take that into consideration.

This is the theme of my life: lead with courage. I was so vulnerable then, I had no idea I was behaving courageously. I was going to have to take a chance and be honest. I put myself out there and let the school counselor know this would be my only shot at surviving. There was no place else to go.

I stood there at the age of fifteen in my warm, watery, shit pool of a life and reluctantly shared it with the counselor.

I can't remember her name but the lady counselor I spoke with saved me by putting me on the list of students who would be placed in the paid program of YCC. All I had to do was show up.

Here is where the "getting wise" part comes in.

I paid a visit to the Social Security office and claimed the money that was rightfully mine for existing. My mother's first husband was disabled, therefore mom received a check for all three children from him. She was still collecting the money even though I wasn't living with her. It was only a few hundred dollars a month, but at this point, that would help me survive.

That check was supposed to go to where I was living. To me, it was like a thousand dollars and I thought, maybe I might just make it after all.

As I stacked my house of cards in a way that any fifteen year old could, there would always be that feeling inside that I had to hold my breath and be vigilant of any slight movement. Or at any given moment it would all come crashing down.

For better or worse, this is something I was good at, thanks to my training at the hands of the people who haphazardly raised me.

I was also good at the Youth Conservation Corps. Cleaning up campgrounds and building fire pits and bird nests was dirty work, but it was fun.

It was, however, difficult on an empty stomach. Lunch was not provided, nor was breakfast. On the upside, I was losing weight rapidly.

I rented an apartment with my friend Shelda. It was a roof over my head, and that was good enough for me. Her parents had an extra bed they let me use. There were no sheets or blankets. I had no dishes, or food to put on the dishes.

Every now and then, Shelda's parents would send her home with bags of canned veggies…which I, of course, would sneak and eat when I could. It was stealing, and from my friend no less, but it was food, and I was starving.

After a full day of manual labor I survived on diet rite cola and mushy spinach from a can. It was only a few months' gig that I had with YCC, but I had saved a little money to hold me for at least a month until I got my next job.

At fifteen and I learned to drink, do drugs, work hard, and party harder. I learned to fuck anything that paid attention to me.

Looking back now, I can't believe how vulnerable I was. All I wanted was to be wanted. There was always that underlying hope that someday a boy would come into my life and rescue me. I dreamed that he would have parents that would love me in spite of the fact that mine did not.

When it came to sex, I had this fantasy of being pure and saving myself for marriage. Ha! Like that was ever going to happen. It was too late; I had already been groomed to embrace self-doubt and loathing. I would never be good enough.

Those were the hopes and dreams of a little poor girl from another lifetime. They were not meant for me. I was taken advantage of and I took advantage wherever I could. I was hungry for food and starved for loving attention and security.

God, now that I see that girl as she was, I just want to grab that child and shake her. I want to let her know that it's not her fault. To remind her that she deserved better. And to tell her that, unfortunately, she would have to create a safety net of her own.

I want to hold her and tell her that as rough as it's been, it's about to get rougher.

Around this time a friend that had moved to Fresno to have her baby (at the ripe old age of 15) had reached out and invited me to come for a visit. It only cost a few bucks on a greyhound bus and my YCC job had come to an end. This was a nice change of pace for me. I needed a break and to get out of Dodge for a few days.

I had earned it after bicycling all those miles to and from work. Then bust my ass all day while other kids had parents picking them up and dropping them off.

I was learning how to earn money but I didn't learn how to handle it. I didn't trust anyone, much less a bank to hold my money. I hadn't yet learned about writing checks or saving money and earning interest etc. So I hid money in my closet, in a hat. I know it's sad, but true. Shelda and I rarely had company so there would be no reason to worry about getting ripped off. Or so I thought. When I got back from Fresno she met me at the door with some bad news.

She had a friend over, but before they left to go out, she found her friend digging around in my room.

Upon my return my trusted friend and roommate suggested that I check my room to make sure that anything of value -- mainly my money -- was still there.

It was not.

It was gone and so was the oxygen that had filled my lungs.

I could feel my house of cards teetering. Why, after all of the struggle, did God seem to think it was OK to allow this to happen? Had there not been enough pain? Had there not been a sufficient amount of abuse? Apparently not, because the hits just kept on coming.

To my roommate's credit, she did try to help me get my money back from the thieving piece of shit she called a friend.

To no avail.

That was it. No food, no money, and no job prospects.

The only person I could think to reach out to was my cousin Dee Dee, who had since moved to San Gabriel, California. As I found out, San Gabriel was barely ok on a good day. On a bad day it was a stinky armpit of a city. You couldn't see the mountains because the smog was so thick. The next Social Security check was just enough to get a flight down, and my roommate felt just guilty enough to drive me to the airport in Sacramento. So off I went on my very first flight, to stay with Dee Dee and her boyfriend in a hole-in-the-wall apartment in the stank hole of Los Angeles.

There were minimal furnishings. A two bedroom apartment with two beds, a couch, a mini refrigerator, and a cooler, but it would be better than where I had just come from. There was no room for me, but thank God, they took me in.

It was a kindness that hadn't been offered to me yet. Dee Dee and her boyfriend Blake wanted to help get me back in school and finish getting an education so that I would have a fighting chance a few years down the road. We worked on that, and on me becoming an emancipated minor.

The emancipation didn't work because I needed a parent signature. My mother was not cooperative when it came to my total freedom. I figured she was angry about the checks.

I had as much stability in my life as an oiled-down slip-and-slide, and the school closest to the apartment didn't help. I turned out to be the wrong color. They had their quota of white kids, so I would have to be bussed to a different school.

Seriously? Too white? That was enough for me.

After arriving in San Gabriel, I purchased a bicycle for transportation . I quickly returned it, and in its place, I bought some home basics: dishes, towels and sheets. I packed them up in a box and bussed them and myself back to where I came from.

I set out to couch surfing with a good friend from junior high school, and I never looked back. I tried to be a kid again, but it was too late. It was a bell that could not be unrung. I didn't belong at my mom's home, or my cousin's home. I didn't belong, period.

Have you ever had the feeling that the breath you just took in may be your last? When I started reaching out for a place to lay my head until I could find my own, I could feel the restriction of air around my lungs. That is the abundance of fear, grief, and sorrow all wrapped in one. It's edgy and raw. Looking back, I don't understand how I ever moved forward.

Thank God for my friends along the way. Even though I couldn't tell them everything that had transpired -- that would make it real -- I could share enough to help them understand why I was asking to sleep on the couch.

It didn't take me long to find a job and a place to live. The job was at a pizza place. Of course I lied about my age. You had to be eighteen to be able to work there.

It was 1981, the year of ``On Golden Pond and Joe Montana (the "49ners")and The Rocky Horror Picture Show. It was the beginning of MTV and, right before our eyes, the shooting of President Reagan.

Life sucked the youth right out of me. I looked much older than I was. I had just turned sixteen. Wasn't that supposed to be the time for prom and dates and studies and drivers licenses?

Side Step....Smiling Eyes

When I was sixteen or seventeen I hooked up with a guy from South Africa by the name of Aiden. He was tall, well built and sophisticated. His sandy blonde hair was purposefully messy and he wore big dorky glasses. He was cute and fun. He came to America on his rich family's dime and wandered into the pizza parlor where I worked.

Actually, I don't think he wandered. I worked with a girl who was also from South Africa. I think their families knew each other and intended for them to date.

She was playing hard to get, so I thought, "Screw her, I'm gonna have fun with this guy."

He was buying my drinks (I had a fake ID by the time I was sixteen) and taking me to dinner. He wanted to go to San Francisco for the weekend and didn't want to go alone. I said I would love to go, but I have no money. No problem, he would cover everything: hotel room, food, and we would see some shows. I thought he meant we'd go to the movies. I didn't say anything because I didn't want to appear as unworldly and ignorant as I was.

We hopped on a Greyhound bus and headed out from my home town of Chico, which is several hours north of San Francisco.

Along the way, Aiden shared some pictures of where he was from and his travels. A seedy-looking guy sitting across from us was listening in and invited himself into the conversation.

I didn't think much of it. By this point in my life, I am used to seedy looking guys.

Aiden asked him for a good place to stay in San Francisco. Seedy Guy told us about a cheap hotel not far from the bus depot, so that's where we went.

We checked in, dropped our bags in the room, and headed out for adventure in Chinatown. It was here that I was introduced to my first taste of curry. It was good and spicy and green, which I thought was weird.

We were having a blast. After dinner, we went to a show.

He took me to a live theater to see A Chorus Line. I was in shock and awe. I had never seen anything so spectacular in my entire life. The energy of the place, and the dancing, blew my mind. I had never been exposed to anything like this.

Because of where I came from and how old I really was, I couldn't tell him any of that. It didn't matter to me -- we had fun together -- but I didn't want to get caught in a lie.

After the show, we went to a bar around the corner from where we were staying. Seedy Guy was there, and he joined us. Aiden asked me to stay there while he went back to the room for a minute. I guessed he was going back for money.

Seedy Guy went with him. I had no idea where Aiden kept his money and didn't ask, but Seedy Guy did. When they got into the hotel room he pulled out a gun and took all of Aiden's money, and his passport.

Luckily, he didn't shoot, but he scared the shit out of Aiden. He was shaking when he came back to the bar.

We went straight to the police. I was thinking, "Crap, I'm gonna get in trouble," because of my fake ID, but it was a non-issue for sure. We went back to the motel that night, and spent most of the next day at the South African embassy.

His family was rich, so they wired him more money, and the embassy helped him with the passport issue. It took most of the day, but I didn't care. I was on an adventure!

We drank tea in the afternoon, and he took me out to dinner again that night, and to another show. We saw Fiddler On The Roof and the following night, Evita. I felt like a million bucks.

In the few days we spent together on this adventure, I learned so much.

I learned about the theater, guns, drag queens, and a new drug that you sniff from a vial. Popper's I think. It was a strange scene for me. I have never had another guy try to steal my date before, until I came to San Francisco.

One thing I didn't know about San Francisco is that it was, and still is, an area hugely populated by the gay community.

It was the 80's and we were in the theatre district of the city. Every bar we went to came with roaming hands and men devouring my date with their eyes. As a female, to use the toilet I went to the "WeMens" room instead of the "Women's" room. This was something I had never expected or experienced.

On the last morning of the trip, Aiden decided to stay on in San Francisco, to finish sorting out his passport issue, and enjoy the rest of his journey from there. I had my bus ticket to get back home, so I wasn't worried.

He walked me to the taxi and we said good-bye. He'd lit up my world, and I was so happy that he did.

It wasn't love, but lust. A lust for him, but also a lust for more: more adventure, more traveling and more of everything.

I was smiling from the inside out. As crappy as my life had been, none of it could take away how I felt at that moment. I will never forget, as I sat in that old taxi waiting to go back to my reality, the taxi driver looked me in the eye from the rear view mirror and asked, "You are Cherokee Indian, aren't you?"

I said, "Yeah; how did you know?"

He said, "There is no mistaking those Cherokee Smiling Eyes". A hint of validation that I was part of a tribe somewhere.

That pizza parlor I worked at was life saving for me. Although it was a double edged sword, because I lived lies upon lies. Thank God they believed my twisted tale.

When I got that job there was no ad in the paper looking for help. I simply walked up to the manager and said in the most confident voice I could, "Who do I have to know to get a job here?"

That was all it took. The short, sweaty, overweight pig of man looked me over and laughed. I describe him as truly awful, but down deep he had a good heart. It was buried under his addictions to gambling and drinking.

That environment was poison to him. Connected to the pizza parlor was a seedy bar called the Chico Chico Club. They held poker games until all hours of the night. When the manager wasn't in the pizza parlor, we only needed to search next door. We could always find him in the smoke filled bar, saturated in greed and sickness.

That job had everything I had already learned to deal with in life. It was the perfect mash-up of sleaze and deceit. I knew how to handle almost every aspect of this setting.

Or so I thought.

In my youth I learned to deal with alcoholics, liars and cheats.

While I was working there, a few family members wormed their way into my ever-so-fragile world. It made things especially tense. In order to protect my story, I had to keep them away. But my family was like herpes. The gift that kept on giving.

Side Step....The Arrangement

I froze as the hair stood up on the back of my neck. The detectives entered through the main door of the old pizza place where I worked and headed in my direction.

Never having good experiences with the cops in the past, I was freaking out on the inside, trying to figure out if I should run or stay and see where this went.

Were they here for me? Had I been outed on my web of lies? Did someone nark on me for working there underage? My God, was it over now? My head was spinning, but I tried to keep my cool.

As they approached, it felt like all eyes were on me. I would lose everything if my truth was exposed. My stomach was turning as I put my guard up. All I could think of was, "Believe you're lie and they won't pick up on it."

The lead detective stepped forward, handed me his business card, and asked to speak about my brother... the criminal. He was the oldest out of the four brothers, and there was no question they were asking about him.

Sigh of relief. I thought, "It's not me. Not this time, anyway."

So what did they want with the criminal? To lure me in and try to manipulate me, they took the nice guy approach. I knew better.

I also knew at any time this could go sideways in a bad way. I calmed myself as best I could and I listened to what he had to say.

The criminal was in trouble. Someone was looking for him. He had been in the wrong place at the wrong time, and now he was in danger. I hadn't seen the criminal lately, but sometime back he did call me. He was looking for a place to hide out, but never said why.

The questions kept coming at me. Where was he? Did I know of his latest transgressions? They made it very clear that some very bad people were looking for him and he would be better off if he turned himself in. If the bad guys found him first, it could be fatal.

There were rumors that my brother was on the run again. I was afraid, because things never ended well for him.

What to do? What to do? Should I try to help him or would it be hurting him?

I took the detective's card and said I would see what I could do.

Later, I put the word out for the criminal to call me, and he did. He confirmed that dangerous people were looking for him, and so were the cops. I asked him if he would turn himself in if I could set up a peaceful way for him to do it. That way the cops wouldn't rough him up, and the bad guys wouldn't kill him.

He was tired of running, so he agreed to meet me at my place.

It was strange to have my brother walk into my apartment. It was a clean space with not much in it but a pull-out couch and a long string of empty Jack Daniels bottles lining one side of my wall. Pure proof of my innocence fallen. Hanging on the wall above them was a Debbie Harry poster that I bought at Tower Records.

To make my brother feel at home, I bought him a few cans of malt liquor. My fake I.D. had yet to let me down. Life had aged me and the photo proved it to be true.

So it was all set. He would stay at my place and I would call the detectives from work and let them know he was waiting. He would be taken into custody calmly, and nobody would be hurt, and the criminal could stop running.

"OK," he said, "I'll stay and drink the beer and wait for the police."

He waited long enough to drink the beer, and then bolted. After going through all of the effort to call the detective and open my world up for possible collapse, he ran anyway. The detective said when they arrived, the door was open and nobody was there.

I had been lied to again, and was now waiting for the other shoe to drop.

It didn't. Not yet, anyway. They left me alone, though the feeling of dread never left me. Who would it be next time? Who would walk through those doors to disrupt my life? The good guys or the bad guys, and how would I be able to tell them apart?

Chapter 4

When I wasn't working, I was trying to figure out how to keep the monthly Social Security checks coming. All 200.00 of it. I had received a notice from SSI that if I didn't continue my education, the money would stop.

This meant going back to school. I contacted school counselors and they transitioned me into a continuing education school.

I worked full time and read books about dead presidents. I didn't care about the people I read about. Those dead presidents weren't going to pay my rent and keep me alive, now, were they?

I was a good student before I was forced into adulthood, but now the channel changed. I couldn't keep up with the responsibilities and maintain balance.

I worked as many hours as I could and drank and screwed anyone who would give me a sideways glance. I was trying to fill the astronomical void in my life. I found myself looking to men for validation.

It almost became the death of me.

That night began as innocently, as any teenage night on-the- town. My friend Barbara and I acquired a bottle of tequila. We took turns swallowing the cheap liquid gold. Just thinking about it now makes me want to hurl. It was a small bottle, and before we knew it, it vanished and we were on our way out the door, walking our invincible teen bodies down the esplanade of our little town, looking for anything or anybody that would invite us in.

We were looking for a party and more booze. There were so many big beautiful old homes on that street, all of them dripping of money and problem-free lives. Or so we thought.

As we walked by one of the grand homes on the esplanade we recognized someone we knew from school. I also recognized a friend of my brother's. The criminal brother. His friend gave me the creeps, and I never knew why until that night.

I had never been in a house so majestic and oozing its history and old money. Too much money. I remember thinking, "Holy shit, I better not touch or look at anything, or it could break."

Who knew, it would be me, that shattered to pieces.

So many painful things happened that night. There is a point when the pain is too much. That's when God reaches down and makes it so you don't feel anything. Even though the body holds memory and knows the level of pain, somewhere it gets shut off for a moment. It's happened a few times in my life. God just flipped the switch so I could continue breathing when I didn't want to breathe. I'm beyond grateful to God for doing this for me, yet it would take nearly forty years to heal from the events of that simple night out.

I would have been okay to end this life at that moment. To stop existing would have helped me not go through more of the same farther down the path I chose. It felt like I was stuck in a bumper car ride without a car to protect me.

There were no fathers, brothers, mothers, aunties or uncles to shield me from these predators. For my soul I have chosen to keep the blog post below in the third person. I owe my soul this kindness.

Side Step....Unbreakable

She came-to with her face in the dirt and grass. The smell of the earth brought her back from where she was. Pain flared in places she never knew could hurt like that before, she quickly passed out again... with her pants tangled around her ankles.

At sixteen, she had no family to take care of her, she went numb. Her physical body searched for love and approval of those around her. She was treading water, and not very well. A fighter at heart, she will survive. She just doesn't know it yet.

She woke again, this time on a hospital gurney, throwing up her anger. Her spirit was full of fire for being treated like the dirt her rapist left her in. She raged, but didn't know why, and passed out again.

Her blackouts seemed to last a lifetime. She woke up on her uncle's couch with vomit in her hair and pain where she sat. It was a mystery how she got there.

Underneath her skin, lived a deep rooted sense of embarrassment, shame and anger. She had no control over what was happening to her. Like a feral cat, this girl was raw. Too raw to be cared for. Yet she was the one person that needed caring for the most.

Nobody nurtured her. Nobody brushed her off, got her cleaned up and fed her. She did it herself.

She was dropped off at her hole-in-the wall studio apartment. Memories of what happened were sporadic, at best. She hurt to her core, but had no choice other than to carry on. That night started with shots of tequila with a close friend. The fearless young girls set off to wander the streets of their little world. What a small world it was. A town of turbulence and chaos where it was all too easy to get lost in booze and drugs. A town where nobody reached out to those who needed the kind of help she ached for.

The freedom of the streets that night, created a prison for her for many years to come. The man that forced himself inside of her troubled young body will never know what he took from her.

Lost in the aftermath was her purse, which told people who she was. The police showed up at her school with it, eventually. They questioned her, but she couldn't, or wouldn't, admit to anything thanks to shame and darkness of blacking out. She didn't know how her purse ended up in that backyard. It had been her guttural screams, the whimpers and cries of a soldier down, that woke the people who lived there. She was found in a way that no girl, or person, for that matter, should be found.

People seemed to look at her differently now. Did they know? If so, how?

No longer who she set out to be, she was now what her environment had created. She was still a warrior, a fighter. The thing that kept her going was the anger and hurt that burned inside. How did it come to be this way for her?

After a period of time, she found herself working and living in a whole new town. Bigger, more forward thinkers. She could make it in the bigger town.

The festering emotional wound that she carried with her had manifested into something physical. An illness in the very place where she was hurt. It followed her. The rapist took away her ability to ever have a family of her own.

That man eliminated her ability to have children. Why? She didn't know.

Eventually the adult woman fought her way through to a more healing time of release and forgiveness. The reasons why no longer mattered to her. The events that brought her child-self to be violently raped no longer defined who she was.

The anger and hurt of the past created the shield she had needed. Now, the memories are there for her as a reminder of her will to survive, like a book she can pull off the shelf, read through, appreciate what they are, and put it back where she found it.

All of the battles that tried to snuff her out never succeeded. In the end, she was the victor. She can view the battle not as a victim, but as a warrior who learned to heal the wounds of the past and embrace the scars that tell the story. Her story.

Even though it's her story, she is a part of us as women. Let us learn from her. Let us reach out to those who we see hobbled by fear and anger. Let us not forget when we see them to ask, "Can I help you?" Pay better attention to those that need help but, for whatever reason, can't ask.

As I am writing through the tears of my past, I figure it's got to get easier at some point. I mean, shit, other people have had it much worse, so who am I to complain? Not much good came out of the family I was born into. The sexual assaults would either come from family members or friends of the men in the family. I was served up on a platter to whoever wanted to partake. Or just take.

True love between a Mom and Daughter

Chapter 5

I received a phone call in the middle of the night from my second oldest brother. Our dad was dead. In a state of shock, immediately I hopped on my bike and rode through the quiet night. It was late and there was no traffic. Life became silent. It wasn't talking back. There had been a death and life had no comment. As I sat by my brother's side, I realized, this was my first death experience. The oldest brother was in jail, again and couldn't be contacted.

Side Step….Brotherly Love

He said he would kill me, and I believed him. My brother was on another drug tear and pissed at the world.

We lost our father and our mother was on the tail end of her second marriage. Not that any of that is an excuse. His prison tats started telling his story. One of the most common tattoos among criminals in those days was "Mama Tried". He had it tattooed across his chest.

He scared the shit out of me, and rightfully so. One fine day, in a drunken rage, he put a machete through the back of our younger brother, very nearly killing him.

At one particular point, he was focused on getting a $150.00 insurance check from our dead father. I refused to sign anything over to the criminal. He was trying to commit fraud and I was not going to be a part of it.

I was eighteen years old and staying with a cousin while I got back on my feet after my move back from Hawaii. The only transportation I had was a bicycle or my feet. I rode that bike everywhere.

I worked part time at Sears department store folding towels. This was just until a full time position opened up at a convenience store. Bicycling at night in city traffic was no easy task. To this day, I'm surprised I didn't get smashed in traffic.

With the odds stacked against me, why would I help a brother who held my life in such low regard? After all, it was his friend that tried to rape me when I was nine, and his other friend that did rape me when I was sixteen. Where was he when I needed him? Good question and one I ask myself from time to time. There were more than just a few reasons to keep him out of my life.

When we were young I loved my brother so much. When I was about 8 or 9 years old I shoplifted candy then shared it to earn cool points. I told lies to our parents and then hid him when he ran away from home. It was what I had to do if I wanted to be around him. Finally, I learned it wasn't worth it and I cut ties with, not only my brother, but the immediate family as well. It was the only way to focus on survival.

My brother went on to commit many more crimes, most of them violent. Often I wondered what happened to him. What flipped that switch in his head and made it Ok for him to do the things he did. What made it Ok to beat someone to within inches of their life. Or to steal from someone who was hard working and just barely making it. Maybe it was his way of pushing people away so he could have control of something in his life.

When he was in prison someone else had control. He didn't have to make any decisions. There was no paying bills, no struggling or guessing where he was gonna eat next. He got free medical and free dental. He never had to suffer with dental abscesses after dental abscesses like I did.

The criminal got "3 hots and a cot" on a regular basis. He became a part of the prison system and once he got in he never really changed from that. Prison is his plan B. By no means am I saying prison is easy but neither was what I went through. Not even close.

So much for brotherly love. There was no big brother protection for me, so there was no need to try again. I lost him for good, a very long time ago. Having already been on my own at fourteen I knew there would be no helping hand from him. He was the oldest of six and all I wanted was someone to look up to and someone to look out for me. Clearly that would never happen.

Some say that criminals become what they are due to their environment. Others say it may be caused by a trauma or intense experience. I have come to learn that it is the soul's choice. Chosen before we even take on the aspect of being human.

In my short years I learned about choices and consequences. You make a bad choice and you will suffer the consequences. It always catches up with you. The more distance I put between me and my brother the more confident I became about making good choices in my life. Better choices led to better experiences and that may be the only good thing that came out of that brother sister relationship.

Lloyd, my dad, choked to death while eating a meal with his "girlfriend." She didn't know how to do the Heimlich maneuver. So, she watched him choke to death. The cause of death was no surprise to me.

To say that Lloyd came from underprivileged beginnings would be an understatement. On many occasions, his parents locked him and his brother in a cage on the back of the family truck and went to the honkytonk to get plastered. It is sick, and sad, and it was only part of his story. Rage lived, and was handed down to his sons.

Lloyd's girlfriend settled herself right into being the lady of a house that was not hers. For me, this became a challenge of who had the strongest will.

She lost.

I got her out of his house by sheer torture and harassment.

Lloyd's worldly possessions consisted of a cockroach-infested house in the worst part of town, a beat up green Pinto wagon and a few thousand dollars in the bank.

I tried to save the house, but nobody would help me. I mean nobody. This baffles me to this day. I walked away with his only photo album, the TV, and my share of the money.

My oldest brother was meant to get the car, but he was in jail, so I sort of borrowed it until he got out.

I had no license, no insurance, and I didn't care. I was tired of riding my bike everywhere, and I felt like the world owed me one. I felt I deserved to drive to and from work like a normal person.

Only, I wasn't normal, and this was a huge mistake.

On the upside, a few months later, I used the car to save a man's life. As it turns out, I had a purpose for existing after all.

At seventeen, I started seeing a bartender/actor I met at an event in town. He was about fifteen or twenty years my senior. He introduced me to a few firsts: Cocaine, all night sex, and my first and last STD.

I could have easily become addicted to cocaine and sex. It was the 80's, and everywhere you turned someone had lines of cocaine laid out, ready for the taking.

I loved anything that could make me go fast. Coke, speed and booze. Little pink hearts, cross tops and black beauties were the most popular pills at the time. I liked it all, for so many of the wrong reasons. Chalk it up to lessons learned and major Karmic clean-ups.

At this time life was showing me warning signs.

I ignored them all.

One night, I went to see my bartender dude. He had a headache that wouldn't go away. He wasn't doing well; He was writhing in pain, and it got worse the deeper we got into the night. I had to get him help. So, I got him to the car and ran every red light on the way to the emergency room.

He had an aneurysm, followed by a grand mal seizure the next day. He would have died alone, and not a soul would have known had I not taken him in. This was our karma, and it would be a quick end to us.

When I went to visit him in the hospital his friends and relatives glared at me, I am guessing, because of how young I was. They began pushing me out, and this was the end of him and me. Our karma was complete.

I soon started getting into trouble with the car. I had a little accident with a bicyclist and my rear fender. It was not completely my fault, but it created a situation where I had to pay restitution. My world began to crumble again.

Looking back, my life was like a sandcastle being eroded by the waves. It felt like life was never meant to stand in permanence. It was a makeshift existence.

I made a decision to reach out to my step-sister Barbara. She had been living with her husband on a military base in Hawaii.

I had never gone to her for help before. Ever. I was desperate, so I asked if I could come and stay with them. She stalled, then reluctantly said yes, but only for thirty days, the maximum a guest could stay in military housing.

I made a plan. An open ended plan, but that had become my modus operandi.

My heart never stopped aching from the lies I lived. I cared for the people I worked with, so before I moved I had to make time for true confessions. I owed this to my current boss and the crew I had become so close to at the Pizza parlor.

I didn't know how I was going to confess to the lies about my age and so many other things.

The fear welled up inside me so much I couldn't do anything but cry the day I went to reveal who and what I really was. I hated lies and liars with a passion, and it tore me up that I couldn't tell the truth from the beginning, but if I had, I would never have survived.

So, that dreaded day I worked, and I cried, and finally the boss pulled me into the office and pried it out of me. I divulged the truth about my age and the trouble I was getting into, and that I needed to leave.

Whew! I said it and whatever happened next, I could deal with it.

My boss cried right along with me and assured me that I had a job there anytime I wanted. Then we went out of the office and let the rest of the crew know I would be leaving for Hawaii and hopefully a happy ending to my strife. A going-away party ensued, including the passing off of the Pinto to the second oldest brother, Gary, who was not in jail.

When I started that job at the pizza parlor, I had just turned sixteen and was engulfed in fear, and uncertainty. When I got on that plane for Hawaii, I was seventeen and had a glimpse of hope for my future. I had thirty days. I could do just about anything in thirty days.

What's that old saying? "Out of the frying pan and into the fire". Dysfunction is taught to us by our parents and passed down the line to our children, and their children, and so on.

Barbara did me a huge favor by allowing me to stay with her, but what I didn't know was that she was in an abusive marriage.

I should have guessed. It's what she came from so that's what she accepted into her life.

I hope it's sinking in: If you are fucking up your life, it doesn't affect only you. You are teaching your kids to value themselves as you value yourself.

I ask you: do you believe this to be fair and just?

As you read this, please look within. Find a way to stop the madness before it seeps out and contaminates the ones you love the most.

When I showed up at my sister's doorstep with all of my worldly possessions crammed into two Kmart traveler trunks, I felt a little lost. Although I have to say my Kmart trunks were a sign of improvement. It was better than the small box and two paper sacks I started with just a few years before. Hey, I was moving up in the world!

To this day I can't remember what I slept on at my stepsister's house. I do know that there had been rules created upon my arrival.

First rule: It was made crystal clear I had thirty days, and then I had to vacate the premises.

The rules were created by her abusive asshole of a husband:

I was not allowed to eat at the same table as the "man of the house." As a matter of fact, I had to leave the room when he was eating. It was a small place, so usually that meant yours truly going outside.

I was not allowed to be in the house if I didn't agree that I would shoot to kill any intruder.

I was not allowed to make noise of any kind when he was in the room unless he initiated a conversation.

Her husband was controlling and mean as hell.

I noticed the change in my step-sister when I first got there. She cowered in a way I had never seen before. I remembered her as creative and full of life as she prepared to go out on her own at eighteen. It was right after graduation that she met her love, her abuser.

Now he had two women to control in his kingdom. What he didn't know is that I was not controllable. I had thirty days, and I had nothing, so I had nothing to lose.

He started on me with verbal attacks soon after I arrived. My skin was thick and impenetrable. You see, I had already been in the trenches. I was well seasoned in this arena. You can try to take me down, but I was a rock at that point. No man was going to fuck me up again (well at least for a few more years). So the abuser's only choice was to get me out as soon as he could.

I learned to get the bus from Wahiawa to downtown Honolulu. I was the whitest person on the bus. It was very intimidating standing on a bus full of Samoan men and women. Everything about me was wrong. My color was wrong, I was dressed wrong, my attitude was wrong and God help me I looked them in the eyes. Wrong wrong wrong. Never eyeball a local in Wahiawa.

I didn't know better, but I did learn fast. Two things of major importance on this island: you need change for the bus and you don't look the locals in the eyes. Ever. I was a haole girl. Nobody wanted a thing to do with me. I did not belong. It was my theme, and as exhausting as it was, I chose it.

Obstacles were not new to me. So, with sheer determination I got a job (door to door sales), a car (a badass red 1974 Chevy Nova with a V8 engine and white interior) and a place to live, all in twenty-eight days.

The only piece of furniture I owned was a twin-sized piece of foam that I used for sleeping on. It didn't matter, because I was never home. When I was home, I was busy shooing roaches off of my counters... Something I had experience in.

I got my driver's license in the local town of Wahiawa. The driving instructor was one gargantuan Samoan dude with a head the size of Texas. Next to him, I looked and felt microscopic.

He took me to the center of town during lunch hour traffic. There were no stop lights where he wanted me to cross traffic. I think he expected me to back down from this challenge.

I did not.

I put my blinker on and not one oncoming car was going to allow a haole girl to get through.

So I fucking gunned it.

The instructor's eyes got even bigger, if that was at all possible, and sweat started running down his face. I literally saw steam come from his mammoth head, and he shot poisonous darts right at me. I scared the shit out of him, but I crossed traffic. He should have never thrown down that gauntlet.

I drove like a local, and I think that is the only reason I got my license that day. I thank God for that V8 engine and my true grit.

It was 1983. I was seventeen and turning eighteen that year. My step-sister never came to visit me on the island. She was not allowed.

I was still a minor child, so in order to survive, I did what I knew best: I lied about my age. I worked hard and nobody cared to confirm my story. I dealt with legal contracts in my sales job. These contracts were not valid if they were signed by a minor.

I was selling a photo-based package. The total value was $700.00 for the photo album, camera and lots of developing, enlargements, etc. It was a good deal, all in all. What do military folks do when they are stationed in Hawaii? Take pictures of scenery and their new growing families, of course. To me, it seemed like a win-win, an easy selling point to use.

My immediate boss taught me how to sneak onto the military bases in order to sell to the boys in the barracks. It was cool because they would hide me when the C.O. would pass by.

My hair was bleach blonde and down past my ass. I was very tan and I never ate except at bar happy hours. I was thin and in relatively good shape, considering I was still developing as a young girl. Looking back, I have so much empathy for the growth of my poor brain. It never had a chance.

I created a working arrangement with the officer in charge of the ladies barracks at the Pearl Harbor naval base. I had to buy what she was selling and she let me sell at the barracks.

I quickly learned that the Army base was a no-go. They weren't interested in spending money. I don't know why, but I think I remember someone saying they made less money than other branches. The Navy base at Pearl Harbor was the easiest to get on, and there were both men and women to sell to. The Air Force base was harder to get on, and not as easy to sell.

My stumbling block was the Marine base. I finally got busted and banned from Kaneohe Marine Corps Air Station.

My boss and I were rounded up like feral cats and put in a holding pen. I wasn't scared. I was pissed off. I was right in the middle of a big sale. The guy was writing a check for the balance, which meant a better commission for me. He was later forced to cancel his contract. Piece of shit C.O. with a power trip took money out of my pocket.

There was never a dull moment living on the island, and working sales was a great way to build confidence in my approach to the world.

When I wasn't working, which was almost never, I was at the beach. At night I hung out at the bars. The drinking age was eighteen back then, so it made my wild life easier.

It wasn't long after I started working that I hooked up with a dude that was more than twice my age. It was the way of this teenage warrior left to her own devices.

I hooked up with the dude purely for sex. I was too young and too hardened to try to have a relationship. I learned all too well that the only thing men wanted from me was sex, so I gave it to them. There was no chase, courtship or romance. I felt nothing at all. It was just sex, and nothing that hadn't already been taken from me before.

So the "relationship" ended when my girlfriend Barbara came to visit from my hometown after I made a trip back to California to watch her graduate. This would have been my own graduating class, had my life not turned to shit.

The graduation was an extremely painful moment. Watching from the crowd, I witnessed my classmates proudly walk up for their diplomas. I longed to share that moment with them, but life had happened to me. Time and experiences were stolen from me over and over, and there would be no getting them back. I was eighteen going on fifty. I could no longer relate to this world.

I watched Barbara swim through the stream of students congratulating each other, and that left me out.

I went back to her house and drank cheap pink champagne with her mother Gretchen. I was forever grateful for her. She had housed me during one of the rough times. Gretchen will forever be in my heart. The good things outweighed the bad things there under her roof. Could I have been guided in a better way? Maybe. Then again, it wasn't her job.

I flew back to Hawaii and Barbara followed for a visit to the tropical paradise. My "boyfriend" was getting in the way, so I sent him packing.

He was an idiot anyway. There is an unwritten rule: never let a man come between you and your sisters. Girlfriends are always your sisters. It was an easy choice for me, so yes, he went away and we laughed, played and danced our asses off.

There are a few things about island life and living in Hawaii that I learned from my boss. For instance, she taught me to never turn your back on the sea, because it can take you out in a hot second.

But the most important thing she said was, "When you land in Hawaii you would either be embraced or turned out by the island. It is a living, breathing thing, and when she is finished with you, she will let you know."

This, I know to be true.

I knew it was time for me to go, because everything was going wrong. I mean everything. The car broke down. I got a ticket and learned about registration the hard way. My job was getting tiring.

I was teaching new employees how to be successful at door to door sales. They were ungrateful and lazy. I was blessed with ignorance on my side. I did the work for survival, not realizing how hard it was. I was hungry and the people I was teaching were not.

Everything seemed to be getting more difficult. After living there for about eight months, I decided to bow to the powerful strength of the beautiful majesty herself, Pele.

The memories I have stored in my heart from this time of my life are fascinating. It is here where the seed was planted: There is more beyond the horizon, and if you keep moving forward, you will find more of what you are looking for.

I went back to California. I called my cousin Dee Dee and her husband Blake and stayed with them in Sacramento for a short time.

It was here I learned about paying taxes. All of the money I earned in sales was not tax free. I didn't know I was supposed to take money out to pay the IRS. They soon introduced me to the ways of being a taxpayer and penalty-receiver.

Seems like someone I don't know is always trying to take my money. Assholes.

Nevertheless, I got a job working at a convenience store and paid off the IRS. I moved into a studio apartment and carried on.

Sacramento was a big city, and a challenge for me. It was more spread out than I was used to. I had much farther to ride to work. It was also far more dangerous than the town I grew up in. It's easy to disappear in a city, and nobody would ever know what happened.

There were no jobs within walking distance, and the bus system scared me. I couldn't even afford to think about owning a car. Cars were for people with money. I barely had food.

After rent, the job left me little money for food. I needed to be able to eat and pay bills. I never forgot the rule "If you work in the food industry you will never go hungry". So that's what I did. I quit the convenience store and started working for a Kentucky Fried Chicken.

In 1983, we had the final episode of M*A*S*H, the Police had the top song "Every Breath You Take" and young girls around the world had the movie "FlashDance."

I wanted to be a choreographer ever since I was little, but that dream was quickly smashed by comments like "You are too short," and "You are too fat." Well, I was short, but I wasn't fat. My dreams were taken away, squelched before I could even try to make them a reality.

When it came to sports or school activities, I never got a hand up from my parents. I wore the same shoes for soccer that I did for basketball and P.E. class.

I was the only team member that didn't quite fit, or so I thought. Looking back now, who really knows what was happening in the lives of the other girls. We certainly didn't have the same stylist.

There was a point in junior high school that resonated for me later in life.

I tried out for, and made, the basketball team, not for any other reason than that I tried hard and I showed up.

My coach was gay as the day is long, and I loved her and her brilliant sarcasm. She didn't take shit from those bitchy little rich girls. I liked her because she saw me. She saw the shoes that I wore. She saw my attitude and my survivor mode and how the other girls looked at me when I moved too slowly down the court. I mean, for God's sake, it wasn't the WNBA. It was junior high school.

The hardest hit came for me when everyone wanted to get team sweatshirts with our names and numbers on the back. I voted against the idea because I knew I didn't have the money. I was outvoted, and so that left me as the only team member that wouldn't have a sweatshirt.

Coach did something for me that forever changed the way I looked at life. She offered me work. If I came and helped her peel wallpaper for a few hours, she would cover the cost of the team sweatshirt.

So I did, and she did.

Coach did an amazing thing in showing me how to get things on my own. I will never forget that as long as I live.

Though the other girls had their sweatshirts given to them, I felt mine meant more because I had earned it. I stepped out of my shithole home and proved that I could earn my way. This was a very important lesson for me. It was a crack of light in the darkness that was my existence.

Chapter 6

I never thought it would be possible, but in the early 80's I fell in love for the first time. He was a musician, and although he cheated and lied, I still loved him.

We fought fiercely and fucked the same way. He taught me more about sex (not intimacy) than I had ever known.

I will never forget the day he showed up with a book about sex. I was embarrassed. I knew I didn't know much about the subject, but I had never had the "talk" about sex or relationships.

As embarrassed as I was, I was also appreciative. He taught me about orgasms, and about cool music. I will never forget making love to the music of Bruce Cockburn's "Lovers in a Dangerous Time."

Eventually, like most musicians, he cheated, and crushed my heart into a million little pieces. It never healed right after that. As it turns out it's not supposed to. That, my friends, is called growth.

I stayed hurt for a long time. I was pissed off about how I allowed him to make me feel about myself.

This is a rhythm that begins from the earliest days in a woman's life. Yes, it starts with the fathers in our lives. I never stood a chance at a healthy loving relationship.

Around this time, I made the switch from greasy fast food worker to ferocious bill collector. I got the opportunity from a neighboring office. These nicely dressed people who did not smell like fried chicken would come in for lunch. I envied them. What did they do, and why couldn't I be like them?

One day, I asked what they did, and was it possible to be trained. Their boss said I could give it a try. For me, failure was not an option.

Not only did I thrive, but I was good at skip-tracing and finding people. It was about "the hunt" more than anything. I earned the nickname Mighty Mouth from my boss's boss.

At this small-scale third-party collection agency, I sat behind a phone asking people to pay money they owed on past due bills. It was the perfect setting for me to vent and sharpen my tongue, and a double edged sword, because instead of dealing with my own pain, I stuffed it or spewed it out on the people I called.

This created a major dis-ease in my physical body. Sitting at my desk, the pain in my lower abdomen was so severe my legs would go numb. Cold sweats and debilitating pain were becoming a regular thing for me. Fortunately, with this job I had something that I never had before… health insurance.

Side Step…. Endometriosis: My Journey

Endometriosis is an unforgiving disease. It affects more than 176 million women, and brings so much pain and anguish it's difficult to put into words if you haven't experienced it first hand.

It was many years ago that I was diagnosed with "Endo." My legs were going numb from pain during and after sex, which was not helping the already dysfunctional relationship I was in. My periods from childhood were so painful I was often sent home from school looking white as a ghost. I would curl up in a ball trying to make it go away.

For me, it was a five year battle with Endo. I was nineteen years old when I went to my gynecologist because of the pain I had been having. He told me he thought I had a disease that I could not pronounce. He also felt what he thought to be a cyst on one of my ovaries. He set up an appointment to go in with a camera and confirm his diagnosis.

I remember riding my bike home in tears. I was scared. I had no idea what it all meant. I was estranged from my mother and my whole lousy family except for one cousin and her husband. I had just moved from my studio apartment to live with my boyfriend, who wasn't, by the way, any help with any of this. When I eventually had surgery, he wanted sex mere hours after I got home. I mean, really, what an asshole.

The first doctor was right, but my insurance wanted a second opinion.

So I went to a second male doctor who told me it would be best to go home and have a baby, and that would cure me.

Stupid fuck. I was angry and scared and didn't understand why this was happening. I screamed at this idiot doctor to, "Take a step out of the dark ages." Asshole! Women are meant to be more than breeding machines.

My original doctor then performed a laparoscopic procedure, followed by surgery every year to go in and burn off what grew back. I stayed with this male doctor for two years' worth of surgeries. Every year, I had to go back in because the disease returned. They couldn't tell me why it was coming back, and they couldn't tell me there was a cure for it. They just kept prescribing pain pills.

Just what every young woman like me needed. Mask it. Cover it up because they didn't know what else to do.

I was getting fed up with not having answers. I was losing more of my youth, and couldn't tolerate it any longer.

I had to have information, and I wasn't willing to accept more pain pills and surgery as the answer. A roommate of mine found only one decent book in the library about endometriosis, and I ended up going to the bookstore and ordering a copy for myself. I knew I would be using it as a guide.

You have to remember this was the eighties and there was no internet to turn to. You got your information from books, and for me, that meant the libraryIt was books you found in the library where you got your information. The one that helped me seems to be out of print, but thankfully there are many books and sources of information to help you now.

I went to a support group meeting a few times, but the women were more concerned about not being able to have babies than actually getting rid of the pain. I didn't want children, but even more, I didn't want this hellish pain.

In the third year, I found a woman doctor with a reputation for knowing about this disease. In the beginning, she did the same thing: cut me open, burn it off, and repeat the following year.

I set a consultation with her in my fifth year because I had made an internal decision and I had a long list of questions that I needed to corroborate what I knew would be best for me.

She explained to me what she knew about how endometriosis works.

Endometriosis is when the lining of your uterus that should flush away each month during your period does not always eliminate from your body. Parts of the lining attach to other organs in your body cavity outside the uterus, and continue to grow.

Basically you have a period inside your body cavity, and the tissue grows and spreads, web-like, attaching itself to your bladder, bowels or whatever it finds, then restricts normal bodily function.

There are cases where women have endo en mass and have no pain. Then there are other cases where you have a little bit of endo and, because of where it is located, it is so painful you can't even walk.

After the last consultation with the more informed doctor (I was now twenty-four), I begged her for a complete hysterectomy. In my thinking, if my body no longer has a uterus or ovaries, then I can't possibly produce more tissue to grow and spread. It was a long conversation, but I educated myself on the disease and I knew I had to take control of my life.

I had the surgery. It was the best decision I ever made. This was, of course, followed up by many years of hormone replacement therapy. I was OK with that.

Now more than thirty years later I see there is still no progress in fighting this disease. I just wonder: if men went through this sort of pain and agony, how far along would we be in the discovery process?

I've been reading forums for women who have endo and my heart aches for them. I answer and comment on their posts to offer advice from my experience. That is all I can do. Imagine: 176 million women have this disease. There is something so wrong about this.

The verbal abuse I have seen on these forums is insane. These are abuses that come from many of the doctors towards their patients. To tell a teenager to go home and have a baby and that will fix things is just plain ignorant. Yes, they are still telling women this very thing.

Who does this? Doctors who are too egotistical to say they just don't have the answers.

This is the point where you have to get real with yourselves, ladies. If children are what you want, then stick it out. That is, if you don't want to use alternative methods to have children (adoption, fostering, or a surrogate). Or, have a hysterectomy.

Now listen, I'm not saying that's your only answer and that it is the right one for you, but you have to do what is right in your heart.

However, staying drugged for years so that you can function enough until you are ready to try to have children may not be right for you either. Remember, endometriosis is one of the leading causes of infertility in women today.

It's not an easy decision, but it's one that has to be made. Talk to as many women as you can, and don't listen to only one doctor. Educate yourself and fight the battle with as much knowledge as possible.

I worked hard at the collection agency, then eventually found an even bigger company to work for. The new job paid on a salary versus commission basis.

I didn't know what that meant, but I learned if I met a certain quota of collected money each month, I could keep the base pay. If I exceeded it, I could get bonus money.

I liked the idea of bonus money. I was hungry for success.

It was while I was at this job that the musician and I broke up. My boss, being an ex-musician, would take me into his office and counsel me through my break up, all the while talking about Country Joe and the Fish.

I loved my boss. He was the shit. He had a stance like the bass player boyfriend I lived with: a John Entwistle (The Who) wannabe. You know, hip forward and to the side to rest the bass guitar a slumped shoulder and cigarette hanging from his mouth.

In the Eighties, it was still OK to light up in the office. By the end of the day there were thick clouds of smoke hanging in the air.

We functioned on an over-abundance of caffeine and nicotine to keep us revved up and collecting. All the collectors had aliases because it was too dangerous not to. My alias was Rickie Shannon. The first name was for Rickie Lee Jones, a cool blues singer with a heavy drug problem. The last name was my boyfriend's.

As bill collectors, we were licensed through the state and governed by the Fair Debt Collectors Practicing Act. There were rules and specific hours to abide by. There were plenty of things we couldn't say.

Our bosses could listen to any conversation they wanted, however we were not recorded. I personally had a few favorite moments that will go down in my collecting history.

I will never forget the old man that growled at me in his thick gravelly voice, "Rickie Shannon, if you ever call my house again, I'm gonna come down there, rip your head off and shit down the hole". Classic.

There was a guy that said, "Now listen, if you are not nice to me, I am gonna take your name out of the hat."

I asked, "What hat?"

"What do you mean?" he said. "Every month I put the names of my past due accounts in a hat and draw from it. If you aren't nice, I'm gonna take your name out of the hat".

I laughed so hard, it made the debtor laugh, too. He kept me in the hat.

For me, It was about the hunt. My favorite find was a guy that never took my calls and rarely, if ever, made payments.

I chatted with his neighbors and found out he liked to play golf. I also found out which country club he liked. Oh, this was going to be fun!

I timed it right, and made the call to the country club. As he was coming off the golf course, he was called to the front for a phone call. Yes, it was me. Now enter the shit eating grin. I didn't care if this guy ever paid again. I had captured the prey and embarrassed him on his turf. It was my best find ever.

In the eighties I remember watching Lifestyles of the Rich and Famous and dreaming of far away places. I had already lived on an island, so why couldn't I visit one?

I loved the tropics. It was hot, and people were tan and sexy. There were crystal clear turquoise waters for miles, and a never-ending source of cocktails to keep the vibe going.

Yeah, I wanted some of that. Bora Bora, located in the South Pacific, was at the top of my list.

I wanted to prove that these places didn't have to be only for the rich and famous. I wanted to prove that the lower level scourge had the right to be there, too.

That was me, always wanting to prove I belonged. It was only eight years earlier that I stood with all of my worldly possessions in a small box and two paper sacks.

The line of separation from where I came from, to where I was at that moment, was not too distant. A part of me believed I was not deserving of these types of luxuries.

I was a bit frightened by the distance to Bora Bora, so I chose to dip my toe in the Caribbean via a middle-of-the-road cruise line.

I bought the sexiest skin tight dresses and short shorts, and packed my bags. I was one of very few singles on board.

I found myself wearing the skinny little recycled ring my boyfriend gave me. I showed it to a couple a little older than me, and I will never forget what the woman called that ring.

"Aw, honey, ain't that sweet? Your man got you a Canardly Diamond."

I didn't know what that was. "Really?"

She said, "Yep! It's one you Canardly see!"

We all fell out laughing so hard we had tears rolling down our faces.

I took it off after that.

The cruise stopped at Jamaica, Grand Cayman, Cozumel, and Playa Del Carmen. Although I didn't care for the herding of people that takes place on a ship, I did discover a sense of wanderlust I never knew I had.

I learned that if I saved my money, I could go every year to a new destination. Work, reward, and repeat.

It was about this time of my life that I started stretching my wings on a psychological level as well. With that first love break up, I needed help picking myself up.

I was alone, with only the ears of my drunk friends and emotionally fraught cousin. She was going through some healing of her own, and had suggested I talk to her therapist.

Ugh. Had it really come to this? I felt like I was admitting I was in the wrong because it was me seeking help.

I sat in on a session with my cousin, and was amazed at the way this guy listened without judgement. I continued to see this therapist, and after the first session, we knew all too well the issue wasn't the breakup. It was about being abandoned by my family and the deeply dysfunctional ways of their alcoholic existence.

My therapist recommended I attend Adult Children of Alcoholics meetings. ACOA meetings were free, and I didn't have to say anything. I could sit in the back of the room and listen.

He also recommended a book, "It Will Never Happen To Me," by Claudia Black. That book pissed me off to no end. I was still angry for what I had been put through. I didn't want to take the victim stance, because that would get me nowhere.

I learned, it wasn't my fault. The many things that had happened to me were not my fault. The molestation, the rape and the ripping away of my childhood were not because of anything I did or said. I know this in my core, but it's very difficult to erase a feeling that is embedded in your memory. The body, as I have learned, holds memory, especially traumatic memories.

I continued to go to the ACOA meetings for several months, along with my regular therapy sessions. Eventually, I got tired of people whining about what happened to them. Fine, this happened and that happened, but what are going to do about it now? How are you going to move forward in your life and take your power back?

Nobody ever talked about moving forward. In these pages, I have started with the history of where I came from to set the stage. I will not end in the same way. It took me a long time, but I'm here now.

When I was going to ACOA meetings, my partying slowed down, but never stopped. I was just like any other twenty something woman finding her way.

Endometriosis did slow me down.

I couldn't have as much fun while high on hydrocodone. Those pills puffed me out and made my skin pasty. It wasn't until I had the surgery that I got my body back.

In 1989, on October seventeenth, at 5:02 pm, during the World Series at San Francisco's Candlestick park, California started crumbling. It was the beginning of the end for many people. Bridges collapsed with people under them. Houses fell apart and California became eerily quiet.

I had a major fear of earthquakes. I knew I had every reason to be scared. I made the decision to move to Washington State.

I moved to be closer to my best friend at the time, and to get away from earthquakes. I looked at it this way:

moving is simple. Put your shit in a box and go. End of story.

What does it matter where you live, as long as you have the freedom to come and go as you please?

I packed up my stuff and stuck it into a twenty-six foot U-Haul truck. I hitched my little Toyota Corolla to the back and drove from Sacramento, California to Everett, Washington. Just north of Seattle, it was a mere eight hundred miles, give or take.

Getting a job was always easy for me. So in Everett, I got two.

I got a daytime collectors job, and a night time waitress job working in a steak/burger joint. It was a way to get quick cash from tips, and I knew I wouldn't go hungry. What was it with me and going hungry? Maybe I had enough Ramen noodles to last a lifetime.

I wanted the job at the steak house to be a social thing. Unfortunately, the only thing I got was the side-eye glance from the locals, followed by "Where is your husband?" and "How many kids do you have?"

This was weird. Like a bad episode of the Twilight Zone. In Everett, it felt like if I didn't belong to a man, I didn't belong. These people had a lot to learn.

The office staff where I worked were particularly snooty, except for the ones that kept trying to set me up. Maybe they thought they could save my soul.

I finally broke down and went on a blind date, doubling with a coworker and her husband.

It was my last blind date.

My coworker, unbeknownst to me, was having an affair with the guy she set me up with, who was also her neighbor. Wasn't that cozy? You bet your ass it was, for everyone but me.

With his lack of manners and complete focus on her, I had quite enough. I went to the bartender for a shot of anything strong.

That is where I met the second, and most intense, love of my life. His nickname was Sonny.

It was a very long time before I knew his actual real name. Should have been my first red flag.

Sonny was good looking, fun, and super adventurous. Also, like me, he hated the cold weather.

The year I arrived in Everett brought record floods and record snow. Seriously, Snoqualmie Falls froze solid. That is 300 feet of frozen waterfall.

Due to icy conditions, I couldn't drive for two weeks.. Trapped is not a good look for me. I went stir crazy, and I made a few errors in judgement. Here is one of a few:

I had quite enough of the stuck-up old hags at the office. So, one boring afternoon I sat in the break room for lunch and noticed the classified ads.

I reached over, grabbed the paper and started reading out loud.

"Hmm... no experience required, servers at Honey's bar."

We all knew Honey's was the local strip club. I stood up and said, "Hand me that phone. I'm gonna call for an interview."

I went through the whole phone call to Honey's right in front of the wretched, tight-crotched bitties that sat in judgement of me. Every one of them single filed themselves right out of the room, holding their breath the entire way. It is by far one of my favorite fuck-you scenarios I have ever been a part of.

Did I actually work at Honeys? Well yes. Yes I did. And their bigger place called Ricks, in Seattle. I won an on-stage waitress dance-off. I kept my clothes on. But every time I hear AC/DC's "Back In Black," it takes me back right there like it was yesterday.

Clearly it was time for me to go, before things went completely sideways.

I loved my best friend, but I couldn't handle the cold. Truth be known, I was falling in love.

I broke my lease and sold all of my belongings in two days' time. I packed my car with my new love Sonny and whatever stuff I could squeeze in. We headed south, driving Highway One along California's coast, until it was time to head east to Sacramento.

If I had to do it over again, I would do it in a heartbeat, because even though we didn't have much money, it was movement and change.

Once we found our way to Sacramento, my old stomping grounds, I called a friend of mine and asked her to put us up. She opened her tiny two bedroom apartment to us. For this, I was eternally grateful.

Sonny was born in Cuba, but he never belonged anywhere but Florida. His family was in Florida, and that's where he felt he could find work. He went back to Tampa With the agreement that I would follow as soon as I could save the money to drive across the United States.

My little blue beat-up Toyota was a gem. I loved that car, but driving across the country through the desert and whatever else was ahead, alone, would be another first. I was in love, though, and would have done anything for this man.

I saved a few hundred dollars and made a plan. I studied the map and chose a route that went south on Interstate Five and east on Interstate Ten. Then, it was a straight shot across the United States.

There were a few little quirks with Blu (my car). Thieves had broken the lock on the passenger side door, so it would never be quite secure on this trip. Also, the radio didn't work. I pulled my dash apart trying to fix that damn radio before I left, but it was no good.

I packed my boom box and a small supply of D batteries to last over the next four days. I wore out my only copy of Jimmy Buffett's "Floridays" cassette tape. I listened to it the whole way.

You are probably asking yourself, what's the big deal? What makes my drive across country alone any different from anybody else's?

It wasn't, until you remember where I came from.

I had never met a single person with the balls to do what I was doing. I still knew people that never left my home town. They had never moved anywhere their whole lives, and I had so many moves under my belt my life was like a damn never-ending chess game, minus the deliberation between moves.

I had zero guidance and support the entire way. No back up plan. I called my boyfriend at the end of each day to let him know where I was in case he needed to look for the body.

Interstate Ten was a good clear drive until I got to Louisiana. I had grand notions of stopping in New Orleans and having a meal. However, it was getting dark before I could get there and these were the days of no GPS or cell phones.

I stopped in Baton Rouge, booked a hotel for the night, and watched my surroundings. There were people casing my car and I had a bad, bad, deep in the gut feeling.

I marched myself right back into that hotel office and said I can't stay. I got my money back and drove a bit further to a small town called Gonzales. I figured I would check in and sleep as long as I could then get back on the road before morning traffic hit.

I'm going to reference the movie "The Sixth Sense," where Haley Joel Osment would have the hair rise up on the back of his neck and the room would chill all around him. This room, this place, felt that exact same way. I had just laid down for the night and I tried to ignore the prickly feeling, but it wouldn't go away.

As I closed my eyes, the noises and energy bursts through my body wouldn't stop. It was like a nightmare, but I was awake. It felt and sounded like screaming souls trying to haunt me.

I jumped out of bed, turned on all of the lights in the

room, and phoned a friend. I was awake. Wide awake and the noise would not stop.

A force bigger than me was trying to push me out of that town. I packed my shit and I didn't walk, I ran out of that hotel.

To this day, with all of the energy work and spiritual readings I do, I have never experienced anything like that and hope I never do again. That scared the shit out of me. Thirty years and counting, and it still creeps me out.

I could not get out of Louisiana fast enough. I have since been back to New Orleans a few times, and it's an awesome city, but I don't go to Louisiana without my spirit team. I don't go anywhere without my team. It's nice knowing they are there for me.

On Interstate Ten, after Louisiana, me and Blu were abruptly introduced to lovebugs.

If you have ever been in the South during lovebug season, you know exactly what I am talking about. I highly recommend pulling over and waiting for them to pass. Save your paint job.

Lovebugs fly around connected by their pieces & parts,

enjoying the best and last sex of their lives before painting your car with their bodies.

I know! What a way to go!

But there aren't just a few of them. There are thousands. My wipers couldn't keep up. Luckily I drove right into a strong Florida afternoon thunderstorm. Lots of lightning and heavy rain ended with the most beautiful blue sky, and rainbow.

Almost as notable as lovebugs was all the roadkill I noticed as I entered the state of Florida. These small animals were curled up like the rolly bugs I used to play with when I was a kid.

I got a closer look and realized they were armadillos. I had never seen an armadillo in my life, and now I was seeing hundreds along the roadside. They're adorable alive. Not so much when they are dead.

All of the craziness aside, I finally arrived at my destination: Tampa, Florida. I walked back into the arms of the love of my life, my hot Cuban lover.

As tired as I was when I got there, I begged him to drive me to the water. I needed to connect to something greater than us. It was late, but he took me to the causeway and I grounded immediately to the warm water.

Having driven from California, I found this to be my new coast. I left my past for good, and I have never even come close to moving back. Visiting friends and family from time to time, much later in life, would be about all I could handle on the West coast. It was the only way I could hold down that iron curtain and keep my past traumas from creeping into my current life.

As it turns out, moving thousands of miles away didn't work at all.

Chapter 7

Sonny and I spent about two and a half years together.

It was love and adventure that brought me to Florida, and it would be lies upon buried lies that would drive the stake right through my heart and break our love apart. He was a backhoe operator, and he suffered from toxins in the dirt that he moved around at the landfill. The money was good and he didn't want to give it up, until he learned by visiting the South Florida Boat Show that he could possibly get into boat sales.

Sonny was good looking and people liked him. There was a guy in boat sales that wanted to show him the ropes in Pompano Beach, further south. I wasn't worried about finding work. I could always find a job. So I agreed to move south with him.

I didn't like our new digs. They didn't feel right. Something was off. It felt like something was about to destroy my universe.

I was right.

Before we get too deep into that, let me share one important fact. When I first met Sonny in Washington, I asked him about previous wives and children. He said he had neither.

While we were living in Tampa, he confessed to having two little boys by a woman who now lived in Missouri. He wasn't paying child support, and to my knowledge, had not been making contact. That changed after we talked about it. He had a responsibility to his kids and they needed to be able to have that support.

One steamy afternoon, Sonny picked me up from work with an awful case of the guilties. Here is where the biggest lies surfaced.

His voice got shaky as he confessed that he had been married and, yes certainly, those boys were his. So how would our plans of marriage work?

When I stopped crying the first time, I said, "Ok, let's think about this. Show me your divorce papers. If you are not together, then show me the legal document that shows your separation and end of your marriage."

He could not do that. He was still married to her.

I died a little inside. This is what lies do when they are told by someone we love.

It told me I was nothing to that person.

It meant they believed I was not worthy of knowing their authentic self.

When a loved one lies to you, they're saying you are less than, and undeserving.

He may as well have slit my throat and tossed me in the bay on that day. He killed my spirit. He killed my joy; my dream.

He killed our love with lies, when the truth would have been acceptable.

And so it was. The death of a love stronger than I had ever known in my life. The death of another family, A family who also lied to me to save face for their only son.

I loved his mom and dad almost as much as I loved him. The loss of another family almost did me in.

To this day, I cannot understand why he lied about so much.

What is so strange is that, on a soul level, I knew that it would end. Months before my move south with Sonny, I sat at a bar having a drink with a friend. She was much older and more seasoned than I was. I had a great respect for her.

She turned to me and said, "You know this isn't going to last with him."

Before I could process what she said, I replied with a nod and said, "I know."

Then, I shook it off. I thought, "No, I love that man and we want to get married and learn to sail around the world on new adventures."

She was right, and I was broken.

It was the end of August of 1992 in South Florida. I called my friends Nina and Dara from Clearwater and asked them for a rescue. "Please come and get me." These were good friends that I had spent time with before and after my break up with Sonny.

Three days after I left, Hurricane Andrew engulfed and shredded South Florida.

There was my confirmation that leaving was the right thing to do.

I went crawling back to my old job in Tampa, where I no longer fit in. My dream of Sonny and sailing and having a family were gone. Yet I still loved the idea of living the Jimmy Buffett kind of life, sailing under the stars of a Caribbean sky.

Clearly I didn't need a man to survive, and well, fuck, I was getting a little tired of these assholes hurting me. Maybe they were right that I wasn't worthy of more, but I was at least gonna try. I didn't have anywhere to go but up and out.

I looked up sailing lessons in my area, and the Red Cross had a beginner's sailing course across the bay in St. Petersburg.

I signed up and met the instructor twenty minutes before the class. I am one of those students. I sit in the front of the damn class, and raise my hand, and I am usually the last to leave.

My sailing instructor was a crusty old guy named Wally Barry. He was a no-BS kind of guy, and just what the doctor ordered, since he was way too old to be sexually attractive and just short tempered enough that he never listened anyones excuses on why they could or could not tie a knot.

If you can't tie a bowline knot, then you are about as useless as tits on a bull.

I learned to tie a bowline knot... and many others. I wasn't fast, but I could do it.

After that first lesson, I floated home on a marshmallow puffy cloud. It felt like I found my way again. I could breathe; I had hope. I could attain that dream I had all on my own.

You know the feeling when you are in your twenties and you have something you are passionate about? Something you can dream of? Sailing was that for me.

Occasionally I would drive to Anna Maria Island on the gulf coast of Florida and dig my toes in the sand. I would close my eyes and picture my sailboat anchored right there. I saw myself swim out to the boat, haul anchor, and sail off into the sunset. It was the dream I went to sleep on, and it was the daydream that hung in my mind at work as I looked out over Tampa Bay.

Our world was changing fast in the nineties. When a disgruntled employee from an insurance company downstairs from my work shot up the building cafeteria and the people in it, I knew I needed to get on the fast track to wherever I was going.

I had just left the cafeteria. Next thing I knew, the building was on lock down and surrounded by police and news helicopters.

They found the guy hours later. He had committed suicide in a park in Clearwater.

Man, did that piss me off. At the end of that day, on my way out to the car, I started shaking. Shock set in. I drove straight to a bar and ordered a double shot of Jack, and a Jack back.

I drank until I stopped shaking. It was January 27th, 1993 and three people lost their lives, and several others were wounded.

I was ready, I wanted out. I wanted out fast.

I needed more experience sailing. I remembered my sailing instructor, Wally Barry, telling me to show up on Wednesday afternoons at the Davis Island yacht club. He said just go to the bar and say "crew needs a boat," and they will introduce you to a captain. I showed up in my cutest lil shorts and tee shirt and got on board my first boat at the "beer can races."

Every Wednesday afternoon, I brought snacks and beer and got a regular spot on a boat. I showed up early, and left only when everything was cleaned up and stowed away. I learned so much so fast, and still it would not be half of what I needed to know in order to do what I wanted to do.

That didn't stop me. I was fired up and fierce with determination. I wanted the dream of living and working on boats.

I met a free spirited boat owner who raced in the races without actually racing. He wanted to be a part of the party but was never serious about the win. I was drawn to this man and I couldn't figure out why. I know now that we had a soul connection from past lives.

We sailed together in some coconut bucket race, and then made love all the way back. He was one cool cat. I will always look back and appreciate him.

But, it was not where I needed to be. I wanted more than drunken nights on the bay. My dreams were bigger. I was building confidence, but I needed to get creative. I needed a plan.

I bought some sailing magazines for the classifieds. I saw ads looking for crew members for charter boats in the Caribbean. I had no idea what that entailed, but I had nothing to lose.

I created a resume and sent it out to a few companies. How it played out in my mind was, they'd get my resume and call me or get right back to me via a lovely acceptance letter. Of course, my head was in the clouds, in love with sailing, and it skewed my thinking, to say the least.

After not hearing anything for months, I got frustrated. I was in Florida, and ready at any given moment. Just pick me! Now!

They never called.

So I said, "Fuck it, I'm calling them."

I picked a company. Not the best of companies, but I didn't know that at the time, and the lady said, "Yes, there was a job."

It was only a deckhand job, for only a week. I was in Florida, and the job was in St. Thomas. I said, "I'm on the plane tomorrow."

Reluctantly, she said, "OK, you're hired if you can get there."

When she didn't ask about my experience, I should have known there were some hidden issues about to be exposed.

I showed up to the crew office in Charlotte Amalie, St. Thomas, with a round trip ticket and forty dollars in my pocket. That was it. I got the introduction to the captain, his 62 ft trimaran, and demented dog Daisy. It was me who had to clean her shit up off the deck. She chased sails and people and the unmoving side of the boat. It was like a Far Side comic strip come to life.

The charter was going to be a weeklong sail from the US Virgin Islands to the British Virgin Islands with twelve people, including myself and a freelance chef. I spent the first half of the week keeping the chef from killing the captain, and she spent the last half of the week keeping me from killing him. This guy was the cheapest bastard I had ever met.

Of course, the crew placement did not tell me about his reputation for being crooked and a grubby slob who hit on his guests. Ugh! There was barely enough food to feed the guests. And the chef, being from South Africa, was challenged by not knowing what Americans would and would not eat. I felt bad for her.

Sailing this trimaran was nothing like what I had been used to at the beer can races or in my sailing class. I didn't know what a self-tailing winch was, for God's sakes. We'd had cleats and brute force.

Tracy, the chef, helped me out tremendously. When the job was done in that week's time I had 225.00 and nowhere to go. Tracy asked her boyfriend if I could stay with them on their regular charter boat until I got another job. I had great respect for Tracy and her boyfriend, Will. They were together and living the dream of working on boats.

They were also well out of the way of the declining safety in South Africa. Coming from where I came from, I knew nothing of what was happening in Africa, north or south. All I knew was how to survive what was right in front of me, and that was it.

I earned my stay on board their boat. I cleaned and polished and whatever else needed to be done. I learned as much as I possibly could and went on my way thinking these guys and I would be friends for life.

I was wrong. We would be friends for a long time, but not for life. They became a very important part of my story -- one I would barely survive. The only thing was that I didn't fit in with them as I had wanted. I was not a South African. I was a lowly American.

I quickly learned that in most other parts of the world, we Americans are often the big ole' butt of most of the jokes going around. We are judged, and laughed at, and never taken seriously. It was simply my issue of trying to fit in again, instead of standing alone, or just being who I am without worrying if I was good enough in the "yachtie" world.

I still, to this day, remain grateful for the good times and life-saving moments that included S/V Majulie and her crew.

After my first season of crewing on yachts ended, it was time to be part of the blowout party scene of race-week in Antigua.

Hundreds of yachts descend on the small island of Antigua during race week, usually held in May. It is the time to party and cheers your survival of a season of crazy charter guests and dramatic crew blow ups. I got down to Antigua at season's end in 1994 and did what everyone else did: started drinking and looking for a boat that was going across the Atlantic.

I slept on the deck of a boat I had raced on a month or so earlier. It was not unusual to sleep on the deck of a boat. As crew, we slept wherever we landed. During the day, we were interviewed by captains for the chance to crew on million dollar yachts crossing the Atlantic.

It never would have occurred to me that this was an option but my world started turning in a different way. I was becoming something different inside. There was a sort of expansion that I had never experienced.

I connected with two guys that chartered Victorious, a 62 foot schooner I cooked on. They asked me what I was going to do after the season ended. I didn't know. I guessed I'd go back to Florida. Most of the crew would be going to Europe or sailing north to New England.

That was all they needed to hear to start teaching me about life options.

These two guys changed my life. In a million years, I never would have thought getting to Europe by sailing across the Atlantic was possible for someone like me. It never occurred to me that I had an option of sipping wine in the south of France, or walking the ancient streets of Italy.

They had done this, years earlier. They told me stories of their adventures, and it got me dreaming.

Then they got off the boat, and reality hit. No way in hell could I ever do that.

I thought.

About a week later, they sent me Frommer's Guide to Europe on Forty Dollars a Day, along with a note to not forget to purchase my rail pass before I get there. I bought a few long sleeved shirts and sweatshirts in case I actually got a crew spot.

On one of the last-chance days to find a boat, I met with the chef on board a Swan 53 called Secret Love. We got on really well. The current crew of five were all men but her. I think she had hope for another girl on the boat.

I think I got that job because of my willingness to work hard, and because Chef Liked me. I would have to share a cabin with only one bed with one of the guys, but I didn't care. We were hardly ever going to be in the cabin.

Holy Batshit, Robin! What had I just agreed to do? My first season sailing would never have happened to me had Sonny not lied and I did not lay down my boundaries. I wanted more... and I was about to get it. No one I'd ever known had traveled to Europe, much less by sailboat.

Captain Chad and Susan were a couple. He is from South Africa and she is from the United States. There were two deckies from South Africa, and one Brit. I shared the cabin with the Brit.

My time at the helm was good. Even with an autopilot, it was exciting. Watch rotated three on six off. Those three hours were split as well, so the first hour and a half would be with one person, then they would rotate off and the next guy would come on. It was brilliant.

I was on first with the captain. He knew I was the greenest on board, meaning I knew the least and had the least bit of experience. I did what I was told to do.

The Brit I stood watch with did not. As soon as Captain Chad went below, the Brit would make changes. I would say, loud enough for the Captain to hear, "I don't think the captain would want you to do that!"

The captain would pop his head up and order the Brit to follow instructions. I didn't want to be a tattletale, but I also wanted to arrive alive.

The journey started on s/v Secret Love, anchored in Deep Bay off of the Antigua Yacht Club in Antigua. We sailed as a crew of six, north and east. We stopped in the infamous harbor of Horta in the Azores, and painted our boat logo on the dock. It is a long standing tradition in Horta. Then we laundered everything that had been saturated in sea water and sweat. Once we got cleaned up, we drank ourselves silly and continued our journey.

Next stop Gibraltar, which is a rock, but is still connected to Spain. As crew, we wanted to take a trip over to Morocco, but my South African crew mates were not allowed to enter Morocco, it being Northern Africa. I knew nothing about South Africa and the laws of Apartheid. My crew mates were white Afrikaners. They were not racists, but they were treated as such, and therefore were not allowed to enter Northern Africa.

My decision was to stand with my crew mates. I opted not to go to Morocco. No regrets.

Next stop after Gibraltar was the Spanish island Ibiza, located in the Balearic Islands. This is where the Captain had enough of the Brit and invited him off the boat. I was grateful.

After that, Palma Mallorca. I believe these stops were for parts and repairs along the way. Things are always breaking on boats. It's been said that "BOAT" stands for "Break Out Another Thousand."

I don't remember staying long, but I do remember what happened when we left. We were headed to our final destination, Antibes, France, where we were to deliver the boat to the owner for his sailing enjoyment in the Mediterranean. However, when we got back out to the Balearic Sea and on our way, we got hit hard by what is called "the Mistral" in the Gulf de Lion. Here is a description from Wikipedia:

"The current name of the gulf appeared at least during the 13th century (in medieval Latin sinus Leonis, mare Leonis) and could come from comparison with a lion: it would simply suggest that this part of the sea is as dangerous as a lion because it has very violent, surprising winds that threaten boats (sailors and fishermen know these dangers very well[1]). This comparison with a lion is suggested by various converging sources: Deroy and Mulon's dictionary of French place names, Mistral's comprehensive Occitan dictionary, Diderot and

D'Alembert's famous French encyclopedia and several texts in Latin since the 13th century."

The weather from the Alps had the boat surfing twenty foot waves easily. We had a good captain who did not want to break the boat or the crew.

I remember poor Susan was freaking out; we all were. She didn't want her watch above deck, which was perfect, because I didn't want my watch below deck. It's easier to get seasick if you stay below decks in bad weather. Besides, if I was going down, I wanted to see everything.

Fuck me, there was a lot to see.

Following seas guided us as we made the turn to tuck in to Menorca, where we were stuck for a week. There is nothing in Menorca but churches and bars.

Going out cost money, so as the only unpaid crew member, I tried to stay back on the boat. One night ended in a great victory for me in a game of Quarters. Finally my drinking experience and all those years of keg parties came in handy!

When the weather finally calmed, we headed for Antibes, France, where there were plenty of yachts and crew. We arrived in the wee hours of the morning, and as soon as it got light, we cleaned the boat and packed our bags. The owner wanted us off the boat immediately. No "thank you" or "fuck you," just get off my boat. I had the feeling the owner was off-the-charts angry because of all of the delays.

I knew my position as deckhand was not paid. I knew that going in. I had hoped for some sort of tip or something. But, no.

The boys got paid as they had agreed to. Yes, that did suck. No, it wasn't the right thing to do, but I think if the captain had the choice he would have paid me something. I packed my shit, hugged everyone, and me and the boys started hoofing it to the nearest hostel.

I had the book with all of the details. That did help, and eventually the three of us shared a Caravan (small trailer) in Biot, France, while looking for other boat jobs. There is power in numbers.

After twenty-eight years of feeling like I didn't belong, there came a point in this trip that showed I was meant to be there. I was meant to be on board this boat with these people at this time. I had courage, plenty of it, or I would not have made it as far as I did. The thing is, in the middle of the Atlantic, where you are a mere speck in the vast space of a living ocean, I found a new type of courage. It was a feeling that didn't come from fear. I was changing my stars. Nobody here could judge me from the mess that I was born into, because they didn't know.

Our lives depended on each other. We were a collective, a fine machine with all of its working parts. We, together, were honoring the idea that we were a part of something bigger.

In the middle of nowhere, you hear only the wind and the water and sometimes the engine. Things become clear to you when you live on the edge of this heightened awareness.

We all survived the trip because we were allowed. The ocean could have swallowed us whole. We could have, on more than one occasion, been hit by a passing ship. They don't watch, by the way. You have to steer clear of them, not the other way around.

We could have been slammed by the tail of a gigantic whale and flipped like a piece of seaweed. There was always the possibility of running over massive piles of floating debris from fishing boats, or floating trash and lines that lay tangled in piles just barely showing above the surface for us to catch a glimpse of at the last minute.

So many things could have come to pass, but God, or the Universe allowed us to make our way. We got the hall pass to cross the ocean with caution and respect.

There was a point about half way that would come up later in my life. The Universe had set a map for me to follow, and I received confirmation I had taken the right turn after all.

Halfway through our trip, the Captain set up a halfway party. He coordinated with a Little Harbor 54, s/v Magic Flute, and we met up in the middle of the Atlantic. I had never even considered this was a possibility.

The crew prepped by dressing in makeshift pirate garb. I didn't have any black clothing except for a black bra, so that's what I wore. We didn't have a pirate flag, so we raised my pink shorts. The other boat was finely dressed in toga attire.

Magic Flute took the lead in a slow forward motion and tossed us a line so we could stay connected. Aside from our halfway part, drinking was not allowed on board. We drank beer and did Jello shots, but nobody was allowed to get sideways for safety reasons.

A few of the Magic Flute crew members jumped overboard and swam to us. So myself and another crew member did the same. Jumping overboard in the middle of the Atlantic ocean was butt-puckering scary.

This was my new world; my new life. I didn't have to wake up in the middle of the night and call the police on anyone. I didn't have to worry about lying about my age.

My age was acceptable. I had been honest about my level of experience, and that was accepted, too.

I was in awe of the whole experience. Dolphins danced with the boat as it cut through waves of bright green phosphorescence. I was in awe of every moment, even surfing down those twenty foot waves outside of Menorca. It was dangerous and, yes, scary, but if I had to go, that would be about the most badass way to do it.

I figured I had nothing to lose and everything to gain. I thought nobody in the world would miss me if I disappeared. This was my beginning, discovering a world that wanted to be discovered.

So sitting on watch listening to the music of the Cranberries and watching Magic Flute drop the line so we could separate and meet on the other side of the ocean was a mystical experience I hold in my heart, an experience that can never be taken away.

It was a gift. I will always sit in gratitude for that special moment.

By the time we got to Antibes, France I'd spent too much money partying in ports. I had to get a job.

Most everyone had crew positions. Pickings were slim, and the French crew offices weren't so nice to the American crew members. I didn't speak their language, and was constantly reminded of that fact.

I finally got a month-long job on a cheap-ass powerboat. I can't even call it a yacht because the owners refused to update anything. Nobody else wanted the job because it only paid eight hundred dollars. It would have to do. I didn't care. I was becoming desperate, so I took it.

The captain and the owners were British. The crew quarters, where we were supposed to sleep, was a hole in the forward deck. In Europe, crew were meant to disappear at night and not be seen or heard. Fuck that. I was not sleeping in that hole with the captain.

So after everyone went to bed, I slept on the aft deck with a sheet.

I remember being docked in Portofino Italy, a place for the rich and famous. The owners insisted on a kosher-only boat and wanted me to serve them canned beans and potatoes on the aft deck. I was so embarrassed. The galley was a shoebox. It was only on Friday nights that the big Kosher dinner was Branzino and rice.

Anyway, it was shit job. I almost quit a few times, but I liked the Captain, so I stayed.

Ed and Gary gave me hope

One night I took the dinghy and set out for the next anchorage, Santa Margarita, by myself. At night it was beautiful. It was risky, because that dinghy was a piece of shit and there was no back up plan, but I had to get off the boat when I could or I would have never lasted.

Chapter 8

When that job ended, I traveled freely about Europe.

I got off the boat in Italy. Florence, Italy rapidly became my favorite city in Europe. I loved the history, and the warmth, and rustic feel of Florence.

This was the same history that put me to sleep in junior high school. It's different when you can touch and taste the elements of the land. I closed my eyes and imagined the Roman soldiers marching their way through the villages.

Then I felt it for real.

I opened my eyes. Yes, that piece of shit Roman had just grabbed my ass. For real.

The men in Italy were challenging. To say the Italian men were pigs would be an understatement. They followed me. They tried to kiss me on the street, and grab my ass in a crowd. These men did not do this to their own Italian-born women. Only to foreigners.

It pissed me off, because I already had my fill of being treated like shit by men. I did not need or deserve more of the same.

I intended to spend a week in Rome to see everything I could. I lasted four days. Fuckers.

I did get to find and experience my favorite fountain in the world, another moment of my past that is forever embedded in my memory, in a good way.

Side Step….Fontana di Trevi

The stifling heat of Rome in August took my breath away. I exited the train station to the barking sounds of men yelling, "American, American!" I promptly replied, "No, I'm Canadian," and kept walking. Of course I'm not Canadian, but for some reason people think all Americans have money.

I was Canadian for most of my journey through Europe.

Frommer's guidebook pointed out a cheap place to stay that was walking distance to most everything in Rome. That was true, but the blocks of the ancient city were longer than I expected, and the farther I walked the heavier my backpack became.

Several blocks later and a few stories up, I settled into a closet-sized room of a large pensione. The lodging didn't matter so much. I wasn't in Rome to stay in my room. It was another stop on a journey of a lifetime. Never in a million years would I have thought this possible, but I've learned that everything is possible if you allow it.

I slept well that night. The next day I took my handy little tourist map and found my way to Vatican City. I was not allowed into the cathedral as my legs and arms were not covered. I had worn shorts and a tank top, as it was summer, and the temperature reminded you of that every day.

I learned that, according to the Catholic religion, it's shameful and / or disrespectful to show the skin of your arms and legs inside the church. However, it is OK to molest altar boys in church.

I wonder if they cover their arms and legs while doing so.

I will never understand this, but then again, I don't understand most religions, nor do I care to.

I had a few amazing days in Rome, but the most memorable day will remain at the top of the list for special moments in Italy. I found my way to the Spanish Steps, climbed to the top, and walked back down to take a drink from the fountain inspired by a sinking boat.

As I wandered the streets that morning, I saw on my map there was another fountain within walking distance from the Spanish Steps. I set off to find it and thought to myself that wandering the streets of Rome is even more magical than I would have expected. It's ancient and beautiful, and I had never seen or felt anything like it in my life.

I meandered down one of the streets and stumbled upon a sort of half-arena. I looked at the other half and there it was: Fontana di Trevi, the most magical fountain I have ever seen.

The sun peeked through buildings and showed off different aspects of the incredible sculpture and flowing water surrounding Oceanus (god of all water). I found a seat on the cement steps in front of the Trevi Fountain (tre vie meaning three roads) and watched and listened. The beauty and sound of the water surrounding the largest Baroque fountain in the city brought tears to my eyes.

The fountain was incredible in itself, but as I looked around, I noticed the artists around me creating sketches of the Baroque sculpture. They were sketching their own version of what Nicola Salvi and Pietro Bracci brought to life back in the 1700s. It's sad to know that Salvi died before it was completed, but that's where Bracci came in. There are plenty of names attached to the fountain, but those two men are not to be forgotten.

I watched and listened for the longest time. It was lunch time, but I found myself unable to leave. My hunger got the best of me eventually, so I went and got a sandwich and soda, then went back to my spot on the cement steps. I stayed at the fountain for hours, until it really was time to go.

I had some memorable moments in Rome and will try not to overshadow them with how the Roman men treat young foreign women. I will leave you with this, though: Rome brought to me the very best and the very worst of things. By far, it brought me the best fountain ever. It also brought me the most ill-mannered men I have ever come into contact with.

Picture it: Rome, circa 1994. While a young American girl sips a cold beer in a taverna, an old man makes a lewd gesture. The young American girl promptly rises to the occasion and throws her cold beer on to the nasty old man and his wrinkly old penis. Of course he didn't get to taste the beer or her, but maybe he will think again before making such a mistake. What a waste of a good beer.

After Italy, I hopped a ferry to Corfu, Greece. I was a young blonde female traveling alone, and that made me a target.

I wasn't afraid. I was on guard. It's a good thing, because while on that ferry I woke up on deck with three men hovering over me and my backpack.

Fuckers. I got loud and aggressive and they went away.

A group of other travelers saw me in action and called me over to hang with them. We traveled together for a few hundred miles, drinking beer for breakfast and pub grub at night. What a blast.

Upon arrival in Athens, all I noticed was how dirty and loud it was, and I couldn't continue to drink that Pepto Bismol pink ouzo stuff that showed up every time you entered a youth hostel. I needed to move on.

I missed the Caribbean, so I headed for the Greek version of island life.

It was my twenty-ninth birthday. I treated myself to a plane ride to Rhodes. I stayed in the ancient city, most of which was underground, in a youth hostel. I wandered the city in the day and quickly grew tired of being barked at by those key-swinging greasy dogs, the male shop owners.

They had a way of leering at you with sweat running down their forehead and drool escaping from the corner of their mouths. They would blatantly undress you with their eyes and not even try to hide it.

It was acceptable to do this to women. I would like to see the handbook where it is written and ruled to be OK to slobber all over the woman of your choice. Who trained these idiots to be this way?

When I had my fill, I ferried over to a smaller island called Chalki with a handful of other people. The combination of rough water and diesel fumes had people losing their lunch all over the place. That would make any normal human hurl upon contact.

When the boat docked, everyone immediately went to a choice of three tavernas. Yes, only three places to eat on the whole island. They were all dirty and dusty because of the drought. I had no idea that a small dusty rock could be habitable. I would need alcohol to get through this.

Just about the time that I learned the ferry would not be going back due to weather conditions, I learned that there was no place to stay.

Yep. I needed an adult beverage.

I met an old man who was casually known as the Mayor of Chalki and the owner of the Taverna to the right of the ferry. We spoke for hours, and he connected me with the cook lady, who had an extra bunk she would rent. She had escaped from her native country, Georgia, which borders the southern part of Russia. In her broken English, she said something about a Russian takeover of her village.

Again, my history was bad, but I was learning first-hand from the people who were in the action. This woman was strong and kind, and I liked her. She walked me up the hill to her house while it was still daylight.

These moments may seem boring to some, but they taught me about want and need. As we stepped up to the cook's house, we passed the outhouse / bathroom. It was a toilet room with a hole, and no running water, because there was no water to be had. There was an abundance of shit, and a greater abundance of flies to feed on the shit.

I quietly held my breath as we entered her home. It was sparse and dusty, but yes, there were two beds in the room. I paid her the money and said, "Thank you. I am grateful."

I kept my bag with me and we walked back down to the taverna, where I continued to drink to be able to get through the night.

When I finally felt intoxicated enough not to care about the shit and flies, I made my way back up the hill to the dusty cottage. I put my bag down, laid on top of the bunk, closed my eyes, and tried to sleep.

The wind outside was so loud, it caused a high-pitched whistle through the cottage. Still, I tried to sleep.

Just as my mind started to drift off, my body picked up the sensation of eight little legs crawling up my arm. I jumped up, trying not to scream and bump into things.

Nope. I couldn't do it.

I have lived through a lot of uncomfortable moments. I had to go.

I slipped out as quietly as I could so I didn't wake the cook. I wandered around the island until sunrise came.

I found a small cement monument with reference to Tarpon Springs, Florida, which is where the Greek Town and sponge docks are located just north of where I had lived in Clearwater. I was amazed that anyone there knew about that part of Florida. I kept thinking to myself, how can a planet so big seem so small? Or was it some strange force putting these things in my path? I was still unsure, because I wasn't quite awake yet.

As I found my way back to the taverna, I met up with two traveling Greek girls about my age. We bonded, and then traveled on to Karpathos together. Their names were Kat and Marie, or as they called themselves, Cat and Mouse. They said I was like a Barbie doll because of my tan and my bleached blonde hair.

Later, I ended up connecting with Mouse on her island home of Aegina. It was stunning beyond belief, with ruins and olive trees and Greek coffee. Then, I caught up with Kat when I found my way back to France. She had a closet-sized apartment in Paris that she willingly shared.

Both were great girls and we three had a load of fun eating our fill of tzatziki, fresh bread, and feta cheese. They taught me about real Greek yogurt with honey and walnuts. I can still taste that tart creamy yogurt, drizzled in golden honey.

From Greece, I found my way back to Italy via ferry, and then trained up to Switzerland, where I found I couldn't afford to spend more than a few hours on my budget. So back on the train I went.

Next stop was Austria, God's country. I stayed in Innsbruck, at a guest house that had down comforters and homemade strudel for breakfast. I was in heaven.

I could have stayed in that house all day just eating the strudel, but I had to see what Austria had to offer. Innsbruck had hosted the 1964 and 1976 Winter Olympics. The slope was huge and amazing, and no way in a million years would I think of skiing it. Not that it was available. I was able to view the emperor's building and its golden roof. I also did some hiking through the woods, and visited the Alpenzoo.

Unfortunately, on a trail outside of the zoo, is where I found out that Austria had snakes. At this time in my life I still had three things I could not tolerate:

1. Earthquakes. I had already experienced too many of those.

2. Alcoholics. Again, way more experience with these than a person should be allowed.

3. Snakes!!! I grew up in the country, so I have stepped over, run past, or crawled around more diamondback rattlesnakes than many a snake lover could wish for.

I must have called on the gods of the snakes, because one slithered right under my foot, mid-step, after I left the zoo that day.

I flew down that mountain as fast as I could, crying the whole way. As I was hiking back to the guest house I carefully placed every footstep where I could see it was devoid of venomous creatures. I said goodbye to my down pillow and comforter the next day and got back on the train.

I had to make a choice: Germany, or Ireland. Both had good beer, but one was close to my heart as it was also part of my heritage. I headed north and west to

Cherbourg, France, where I caught the ferry to Rosslare Harbor, Ireland.

Everyone on the ferry started out playing music and Irish jig dancing, then the ride got rough and all hell broke loose. The air quickly filled with the stench of beer and barf.

I had been in rough weather, but due to the convergence of currents and wind, this was the choppiest. It was nasty, but I knew it couldn't last forever.

Once we pulled in to Rosslare Harbor, I knew my funds were dwindling and I had to make this my last week. Also, it was October and it was starting to get cold.

I stayed a few days in Cork and bought myself some overpriced Levis jeans. I went on to Galway and met the nicest people ever. This is also where I started noting the sounds of people from another place, not of this world, and had my first full-on spirit encounter.

In Galway, the first guest house I stayed at was haunted. Nobody said I should expect to hear a chatty little boy in the middle of the night, but I did.

I'd come in from a full day of roaming about Galway eating fish and chips and staring at the beautiful seaside full of periwinkles and bright green moss. As always, I hit the pub before ending my day, but I didn't get drunk, just comfortable.

I walked up the creaky stairs to my "attic" room feeling pleased about my day of walking around my ancestral homeland. Wouldn't my grandma be proud of me if she knew?

I laid my tired body down and I closed my eyes.

That's when I heard the exuberant chatter of a little boy, so excited that all of his words were mashed together.

I couldn't understand what he was saying, but I could feel his three year old self bouncing off the ceiling with excitement, wanting to tell me everything he knew in about a half a second. It was like all of his words were on a loop. He was giggling and so happy I could hear him. The boy was beside himself with delight.

As far as I remembered, this was my first experience of otherworldly conversation. The boy wouldn't shut up, and I was exhausted, so I sat up in bed and said, "You have to stop! I need sleep or I won't be able to function tomorrow. Please calm down and let me sleep."

He did.

I never heard another word, and I never told the hostess, but I'm sure she was already familiar with the boy.

The rest of my trek through Ireland was amazing, except for that one moment I caught a news story while eating breakfast in Dublin.

Remember, this is before iPhones and the information era, and I hadn't been watching TV or listening to news stories. I had no idea what was happening in my country or what was in the news cycle. Those were the days.

Apparently, a car chase featuring a white Ford Bronco and a murderous ex-football star were more important to my country than anything.

Ugh. So embarrassing. These are the moments I chose to say I am Canadian when people ask. I mean, really, who wants to be associated with these ridiculous events? Show us when you put these guys in jail, not when you are chasing them down the highway, glorifying the idiots.

I started that otherwise placid and misty morning seeking to be a part of something more valuable, so I caught a bus to Powerscourt Estate. I got off in Wicklow County at the entrance and walked the beautiful tree-lined, foggy road that led to the estate. I had never heard of Powerscourt, but was so glad I experienced it in this way.

Construction began on the house in 1731 and finished ten years later. Unfortunately it took damage from a fire in 1974, and was closed at the time of my visit in 1994. It wouldn't open until 1996, after it was reroofed and put back together. I missed the house, but the gardens were enough for me.

I went on to recognize this estate in movies over and over again. Apparently it's been used as far back as 1944, in Henry V with Laurence Olivier. My favorite movie filmed at Powerscourt will always be The Count of Monte Cristo.

It may seem like nothing to most people to see a mansion on the big screen and say, "Hey I've been there," or "I have walked those grounds," but it's massively important for someone like me. I'm that small town girl who didn't mean anything to anybody. I was overlooked in school halls and family gatherings, but now find myself seeking to belong in the world, rather than trying to earn the approval of people who wouldn't embrace me as a human deserving of breathing the same air.

My world was getting bigger. The universe was expanding my outlook and showing all of the possibilities. This is important for you to take in. Please remember there may be a notable moment in your life when you share with a young person how much more there is to experience in the world. Remind them to step into the world and its challenges. Remind them they are worthy of being a part of anything they choose. Only they must choose.

Hmmm, go back to Florida for the summer or sail across the Atlantic and backpack through Europe where the Ancients have walked? I had choices that I never knew were mine to make. Nobody in my family ever said that one day I could sail through the Straits of Gibraltar, where many ships have passed for centuries.

It's all because someone suggested to me that there were options; that I had an option.

I placed my bare feet upon ruins built thousands of years ago, which reminds me that those who abused my physical body had zero control over my soul. Looking back now, I remember feeling that I couldn't believe where I had just been, and that made me feel changed as a person. If I had to die at that moment, nobody could ever take away what I had just experienced.

It wasn't but a few weeks and a few temp jobs after my walkabout that I returned to the Caribbean to start the new charter season as a stewardess deckhand on yachts. I got a job.

It wasn't a great job but it gave me a place to stay and a boat for the season. I didn't like the Captain. He gave me the creeps. He was not the first Captain I would work for that would take the boat away from the docks so the crew wouldn't be able to jump ship for a better position on another boat. It was a common occurrence, as was the Captain telling people he and the cook/stew were a couple.

Men can be such fuckers. Not all men, but Jesus H. Christ, there are way too many of you guys out in the world pushing people around with your dicks.

It makes me sick. True power lies in integrity, and there is no integrity in leading with your dick.

I worked the St. Thomas boat show that year and hoped for change.

I got a change that took my life.

Sitting on the jetty wall in Horta, Azores

Chapter 9

I fell victim to the propeller blade of a faulty outboard on the dinghy associated with the boat I was crewing on. It sliced up the left side of my face, the power of the blade shoving my teeth into my sinus cavity. My left orbit -- eye socket -- was fractured, and the wall it sits on. My left retina was torn from the iris, leaving me with a kaleidoscope view from that eye. One of the five nerves that control facial movement was severed, never to be reconnected. My left ear was shredded, and my left arm was nearly severed between the elbow and wrist.

Side Step....The Transition

I'm not wet, but I'm floating

Floating without a face below the sea

Silence, peace is all that I hear

I can feel no more pain, no more fear

A hand is there

Hanging down from nowhere

It just is, it just was, it will always be

Summoning me over for safety

For breath where there is no oxygen

For hope where there is no more existence

For a moment of clarity

That its not the end, it's the beginning

The bright light shines on my soul

I float to safety in the strength of this massive hand

The embrace, like a child to its mother

Hang on, you'll be OK, I hear it say

No words spoken

Here I float completely broken

Shredded and torn

Weathered and worn

This is my awakening, my true beginning

My forgiveness, who knew?

Who knew?

I was taken to the hospital in St. Thomas. The surgeon on call was informed of the accident at 11:30 that night. He didn't show up until 7:30 the next morning. So much for the Hippocratic Oath.

I spent two weeks in the hospital swollen and leaking fluids out of my face. I couldn't eat and could barely drink. If it weren't for the other yacht crew bringing me nutrient drinks and tissues, it would have been much worse.

At one point, there was a question of whether or not I had insurance. The captain I worked for was responsible for my safety, and he had fled the island because he thought I was going to try to sue him for his boat. Idiot. Finally, he was found and brought back to confirm my coverage.

Nobody would touch me until then. So I laid in limbo, struggling to survive.

Before I could look in a mirror, I was taken to the depths of the hospital to have an eye surgeon assess the damage to my left eye. As I was rolled down the hall and through a waiting room, a little girl looked at me and screamed.

My face scared her.

Shit, my face scared me too. But this made my stomach sink to the pits of beyond. I will never forget the moment I looked so horrible I frightened a child.

She screamed and wept.

The doctor, in all of his years of experience and wisdom, took a look at my eye and said, "Yep, you are gonna be OK."

Fuck.

I had to get out of this place before I died again.

It was days before I was able to get a look at my new face. My friend Tracy walked me to the shabby little mirror in the bathroom. I was swollen beyond recognition. Yellowish fluid seeped from the hole in my face. I couldn't speak well.

I had physical and emotional pain beyond what should ever be felt. I moaned more inside than outside. I felt shame and embarrassment, even though it wasn't my fault. Why had this happened? Why was it necessary to inflict more pain onto me than I'd already experienced

Would my peers accept me, like this, into this wonderful new world I had just found? Or was it being torn away from me because I didn't deserve it?

I had a hard time holding myself together. So many emotions raced through my mind. I didn't know what to think.

The hospital ran out of pain meds. They didn't bathe the blood off my body or out of my matted hair. I had no clothes, because the captain left with all of my belongings. My friends, Will and Tracy, helped clean me up and get me semi-functional. I had visits from several other crew members. They had to work as well, so their visits would ebb and flow.

I remember not being able to sleep. One night, I was walking the halls and made my way down to the emergency room to thank the sole nurse on duty the night I was brought in.

Yes, that night there was one nurse. He, with the help of Will & Tracy, helped get me into the CAT scan tube, and kept me from flailing off the table. I remember throwing up all over them, a reaction to a shot I'd received. I remember my clothes being cut off.

That was it.

Except for the traveling nurses and visiting yacht crew, I wasn't really checked on a lot in that hospital.

A day or so after the IV was placed in my arm, it slipped out of place. My arm blew up with fluid, and by the time anyone noticed, my skin became so saturated it came off with the tape holding the tube in place.

My ninth day in the hospital was Christmas, and the staff had their celebration on. It was the Caribbean, where the attitude is, "Keep the rum flowing."

I heard music blasting from the break room across the hall. I got up and saw the food and med trays sitting there waiting to be distributed to patients. It would happen eventually, but first, it was time for cocktails. Let the rum drinks flow. Yes, they were drinking on duty. I couldn't eat, so I didn't care about the food, but what about the rest of the patients?

I had to get out of that hospital. It was becoming more dangerous than the actual dying I went through to get there..

I had friends back in Florida trying to get me transferred, but it wasn't going to be easy. I would have to fly in and go through the emergency room. My yacht friends got together and got me a ticket back to Tampa, where other friends picked me up at the airport.

My biggest fear was seeing the reactions of friends who hadn't seen me yet. It cut right through my heart. Horror and pity came to mind.

Very quickly, I learned to pretend it didn't bother me. What helped me the most was, we broke down on the way to the hospital. It was hysterical. Although I hurt and I was shredded inside and out, I didn't care, because I knew help wasn't that far off.

That laughter helped me get through the next shock: receiving the real diagnosis, where I was told the entire story of what my physical body had been handed in this accident.

In St. Thomas, I was told I would never smile again due to nerve damage.

I should have been told that even though my face won't move the same, it won't prevent me from smiling on the inside and outside.

They could have said that my spirit is so resilient, people will feel my joy before they see it on my face.

None of this took place. I lived with "you will never be able to smile fully again".

Out of the thirteen surgeries I had as a result of the accident, the first and most important was the retinal reattachment, which would require me to sleep sitting up for a month… until we could do the next surgery, and the next, etcetera.

During this time, I struggled with depression. I was staying with the friend I'd lived with before I'd left for the charter season that year. After a while, she grabbed me by the arm and warned me, "Now is when you have to make the choice to survive. If you don't fight now, the depression will take over, and you won't make it."

It scared me straight.

The yachties in St Thomas had a fundraiser for me. This was unexpected, and a blessing, all at the same time. I had no money and no idea what I was going to do. They called me during the event and my favorite local group, Dick Solberg, AKA the Fiddler and the Sun Mountain band, played my favorite fiddle tune, "South Wind."

I cried for the song, and I cried for my situation.

That event afforded me the money to go to California and visit with friends while I healed.

I was now a thirty year old woman with disfiguring scars on her face and body. What man would ever fall in love with that? I would never feel that part of my face. My eye would never be the same, or even close to what it once was. I was changed forever.

An eight year legal battle to follow, and all those surgeries to go through, could not alter the facts as they stood at that point.

It was not easy entering back into the charter yacht season. I looked different. I was different. I didn't want to give up what I had found working and living on the water. I did day jobs cleaning boats and small construction jobs until I landed my next boat job.

It was a shitty little powerboat, but with a very cool captain with similar scars as me. Thank God for that. We looked like two pirates waiting for the next pillaging to begin.

I have so many stories of that boat, most of which need to be told over several drinks, and I haven't had one yet today. Captain Phil, you gave me a chance when I didn't think I had one. Thank you, wherever you are.

I continued to work on boats and fend off judgements from crew who would say nasty things behind my back, both about me and the accident. Most of these had to do with me being a woman and relatively new on boats. The hits just kept on coming. I was shocked, but kept my head down and pretended like I belonged with the best of them. It's not how I felt, but I had already been taken down so low in my life that this was simply a part of my normal.

I worked on boats, and in between seasons I went back to Florida to get the surgeries that needed to be done. My face was rebuilt with titanium mesh and screws. I had to heal enough before going back each season to work some more. Although I had some limits, I just kept working.

It's all I knew to do.

Side Step....Band of Gold

There is no better feeling than knowing that where you are, is where you are supposed to be. I've had many moments throughout my life when I truly knew I was right on track. One such moment happened while I was working down in the islands on a Little Harbor 54 sailboat named Pentoga, named for an Ojibwa indian chief's wife.

The captain and I were sailing the owner and his wife from St. Martin to the British Virgin Islands. We went through the Anegada Passage from St. Martin to Virgin Gorda. Now, if we were going the other way, it would be called the Oh-My Godda Passage due to the way the currents converge in that area, resulting in some very nasty wind and swells.

Luckily for the owner's sake, the wind and seas were following, which truly made for an awesome sail. We were sailing at night, with the captain and I taking three-hour watches.

This was a crystal-clear night, not a cloud in the sky. It will go down as one of the more memorable sails for me. It was the night I married myself to the sea.

I was up on deck, on my watch, sometime in the middle of the night. The warmth of the night air and salt water on my skin felt so comforting. I listened to the rush of water on the hull as the wind and waves pushed us through the sea with ease. There was so much beauty and so much power, the feeling was unforgettable.

I was wearing a gold wedding band that my mother gave to me from her first marriage. While that marriage didn't last, I knew in my heart that the gold band could be used to represent something bigger than that.

To me, the sea represents freedom, life, love and adventure. It is all-knowing and powerful. It can carry you along in its loving embrace, or it can pick you up and flick you across its body for miles like the little speck that you are. I love what it represents, and I want the sea to always be a part of who I am.

So on this magical night I sat up on the deck of this sailboat in the middle of the Caribbean and married myself to the sea.

I used the gold band as an offering, and made a promise to always respect, love and honor what the sea is to me. In turn, it will always take care of me. Even in the worst of storms, I will always be protected.

I've only told a few people about this moment, until now. I share it with you because it's part of who I am. Not everyone understands that to throw a gold ring in the sea means more than the value of the ring itself. Just like a marriage, it's about the pact, the promise to honor and respect the one to whom you made the pact.

I find peace in the salt water and feel like it's a part of me forever.

There are no words to describe the comfort it brings me to be in its embrace, no matter what part of the world I am in. It will most probably be my most profound love in this life. So as I am now so far away from where I made this pact, I find myself dreaming about this moment and planning my way back to my comfortable place: the home in my heart I call the sea.

One season, while waiting in Charlotte Amalie for a boat I was scheduled to work on, I met a boy (all men are boys to me). This man/boy and my captain were both from the same home town, Padanaram, Massachusetts, a coastal village near South Dartmouth. He was a few years younger than me, but he was cute, and he didn't scoff at my scars.

I was terrified of meeting anyone because of the way my face looked and felt. Would I be able to kiss? Would my disfigurement squelch my chance at romance?

Of course the urge was there, but the underlying fear wouldn't stop screaming at me. My fears didn't stop him from pursuing me. I think he liked me because I would fit on his boat and I had sailing experience.

His brother was his only crew and they had just sailed down from Massachusetts. He would soon be on his own. He was looking for a girl, but he was not stupid; he needed a girl that could sail as well.

I have to admit I fell hard and fast for Chris. He would turn out to be my third love.

It was my second season working for the owners of s/v Pentoga, a Little Harbor 54 that used to be called Magic Flute -- the very same boat I swam to in the middle of the Atlantic in May of 1994. I was a big fan of the owners. Unfortunately, this time around my captain was taking a turn for the worse, drugging with people on the boat that didn't care about the boat or its owners. They only cared that they had a place to party.

I didn't like it, and I didn't want to be a part of it, so I jumped ship. I landed right on board s/v Charis with Chris, and we sailed off into the sunset... sort of. We sailed around the British Virgin Islands, making our way to race week in Antigua at the end of the season with all of the other boats. This is where everyone departs across the Atlantic to Europe or up north to New England, or better yet, through the Panama Canal. I was half-heartedly looking for a boat to work on, and Chris was looking for a crew to sail back home with. Needless to say, I didn't want to see him sail off with the female crew, so I agreed to sail at least to Bermuda, and then his brother could fly and meet him to help with the sail back home.

All things considered, I think we did well sailing offshore together. I gained trust in him and I believe he grew to trust me. I could be wrong on that last part, but at least it felt like I was good for him offshore when it came down to it.

The closer we got to shore, the more he would remind me how much he knew and how much he thought I didn't know. That's what it felt like, anyway.

Chris and I would sail many miles together, but my insecurities and his need to control his "investment" would be a big problem with that relationship. Chris always felt different, or like he didn't belong because he was a "liveaboard" in his hometown. But I don't think people were staring and pointing as much as he thought they did.

We were together for about four years. One season, we sailed together from Padanaram, Massachusetts down to Bermuda. Then Bermuda to Philipsburg, St. Maarten, and on down throughout the Caribbean. We made it all the way to Grenada before heading back north.

Things got really tricky in the beginning of that trip.

Side Step....Green Water

The destination was south by way of Bermuda, leaving through the southern entrance of Buzzards Bay. It was 600 miles to Bermuda, and much farther to the more southern islands. Just Chris and I aboard s/v Charis. I had every faith in Charis and trusted him with my life.

We sailed through the South side of Martha's Vineyard where JFK junior's plane went down, which was very sad and very powerful. The beginning of our sail was a little rough, as it always is when sailing close to the shore. The convergence of sea, land, currents and wind can act a bit like a washing machine. It smoothed in the night, but still held the October chill.

We sailed well together, he and I, on his boat. Charis was always his boat, his home, and that was never to be forgotten. He knew her inside and out. He knew what made her tick and how to fix any of her ailments.

Too bad he never tuned into me that way.

The fridge was stocked with food and block ice. It was layered accordingly, with one pot wonders on top for offshore meals in the pressure cooker. About 300 miles into blue water we hit a calm. There was no wind, but there were these back eddies in the water. We were crossing over the Gulf Stream, the massive current that flows from the South to the North. It holds enough power to push even the biggest boats off course.

I had the most unexpected feeling of "the other shoe dropping." The silence was sickening... until a heart-stopping sound came from below.

It was the bilge alarm, which meant the boat was taking on water, and fast.

Chris yelled, "Take the helm," and flew below with lightning speed.

Fear enveloped my entire being. As he crashed and banged below decks, I prayed above deck. The engine vibrated so violently, a hose came off the stuffing box.

This is not a small problem. This is a massive could-sink-your-boat-in-a-second problem. I don't know how, but by the grace of God, he did it. He fixed it in a macgyver type way with some inner tube and putty of some sort. We weren't sinking any more.

He saved us from climbing up into the life raft that day. However, this problem left us without an engine. There was no choice but to keep it old school for the rest of the trip. It was another 300 miles give or take to Bermuda and there was no wind for our sails… until that night, the wind picked up. Happy to have the wind moving us forward, we had no idea what was coming next.

He did all of the right things before leaving Dartmouth. Weather reports and Bob Rice's weather windows for offshore mariners (Bob Rice studied weather, and when weather windows would come up, he would notify those that paid him for his services. He helped the sailors who didn't have all of the latest technology locate their window of opportunity to get sailing offshore).

This was October in the Northeast, and it was either cold and nasty, or colder and nastier, it depended on the day. We got our window of opportunity and left. However, what is the old saying?

"Man makes plans and God laughs."

After surviving almost sinking, we thought we could get through anything and that we were well-protected. We were right in saying well-protected, but that didn't mean we weren't going to be challenged.

Having only a few years (mostly offshore) of sailing experience, I could hold my own, to a point. It took a lot to shake me from owning the task at hand. He had many years of sailing experience under his belt, mostly in New England. This is where the term Nor'Easter would send shivers up anyone's spine. What we were sailing into, nobody could be warned of.

The weather picked up that night, and even more so the next day. We were able to make headway, but not without reefing the mainsail to less than half, and the storm sail to only a small triangle. This means that there was so much wind, if the entire sail was up it would either rip to shreds or knock the boat on its ear.

The closer we got to Bermuda, the worse the storm was. Later that day, Chris got on the single side-band radio and touched base with a ham radio operator by the name of Herb Hilgenberg of Southbound II fame.

Herb operated out of Canada, helping Mariners with offshore weather info. Herb was serious. Once you checked in with him, he had you in his sights and would follow you through as far as he could. We got on his list of check-ins.

He told us there was a massive convergence that would be a danger to all mariners in that area. He didn't say this, but it was a hurricane that wouldn't be named because of how it came together. We weren't alone in this massive shitstorm, but that didn't make us feel any better. We were advised to "heave to" until the system passed. That meant to basically remove all sails (which we had already done) and ride it out with the helm locked down.

To help put this into perspective, we were in a space of thirty-five by nine and a half feet and we were double-harnessed into the cockpit. The cockpit of this boat had no dodger for protection from weather except for a turtle hatch above the companionway.

Which is fine if you are in good weather. We were not. There was no protection from wind or rain or waves. There was nothing to break the view from behind us.

These were, by far, the biggest waves I had ever seen in my life. They were at least twenty-five feet and breaking. The waves were following at one point and then as the weather moved, it put them on our beam (our side). We tried our best to quarter up the waves and hang onto our asses coming out the other side.

After twenty-four hours of this, it was beginning to wear on all three of us: him, me and the boat. The whole time, during this storm we knew the repair could come undone and that would be that. There would be no recovery from this.

Eyeballing the distance to the life raft and where the on-deck knives were, I had a plan if I needed one, and I'm sure he did as well.

Then, out of nowhere, in front of God and everyone, a rogue wave lifted us up and put us on our side while all of its mass poured over the top of us.

He and I were literally standing up on the side of the cockpit, feet on one side and head on the other, hanging on to whatever we could find. There was nothing but green water everywhere.

This means we didn't just get the top of the wave over us, we got the whole enchilada. Which is why it had the power to do what it did. Charis may be a smaller boat, but she draws six feet and she was heavy, and weighed down with all of our stores for the trip. There was power in that wave. This is where I learned the term "green Water."

We only lost a few things overboard. Thank God for our harnesses, our sheer strength, and our will to live. It was at that moment we looked at each other and started making plans for our land jobs if we made it out of that mess alive.

That night, he made another effort to contact Herb on Southbound II. Herb said if we had a sea anchor (a parachute that is attached to the boat but thrown overboard to slow the boat from getting pushed off course) to put it out; that things weren't quite finished. It would be more than forty-eight hours that he and I and Charis were hove to before things started to settle down enough to put a little sail up. We could handle the ten to fifteen foot seas that remained.

We finally made good progress towards Bermuda. However, the channel into St. Georges was narrow and unforgiving without an engine. This meant we needed all of our wits about us… well, about him anyway.

We had gone way too long without sleep. So, in order to make the approach, he had to rest. He went below and I sailed in circles. Now, I don't know if he ever got any sleep, because I had to sing to keep myself awake. I can't carry a tune to save my life, but it helped me keep my eyes open.

As the day grew brighter, we headed for St. Georges cut. He sailed us through, and luckily, the sides of the channel didn't block all of our wind. We were exhausted and elated. We dropped the hook (set the anchor) and had to rest before putting together the inflatable dinghy and checking in to immigration.

We learned that the storm had dismasted sailboats and threw some crewmen overboard, and that there were a few mayday calls to the Coast Guard. I can't explain the feeling of gratitude and awe that I felt having survived that massive force of nature. The winds were clocked at close to seventy miles per hour, and that was just six feet off the deck. The sound of the wind from that storm will be forever embedded in my mind. We were simply a tiny speck of nothing compared to what had surrounded us.

Trying to walk on land after having been through that was hysterical. It didn't feel like land at all. Every time I went to put my foot down, it seemed like there was nothing there for it to touch. It felt like I was trying to walk on top of a tub full of bubbles.

After regrouping and touching base with other sailors and a repair shop, we couldn't fix the engine problem in Bermuda. This meant only one thing… raise our sails and get used to tacking our way south. Destination: St. Maarten, and so it went, and so we went.

It would be after this amazing journey and its ups and downs that we hunkered down for a bit in Newport, Rhode Island while Chris took an architecture job and I worked at the now-famous Mad Hatter Bakery with Audra Lalli.

Chapter 10

There was snow on the ground and we were living aboard his boat. I was continually reminded: it was his boat, his dinghy, his kayak. His family, and his friends. Fuck, his his his.

So we started having conversations about getting a second boat together. We could keep one boat in the Caribbean and cut out the commute. We would simply fly down each season and still have that liveaboard life.

The search was on. Finally I found a sister-ship to his boat Charis. It was a good idea, but I don't think he meant it. Owning something with someone scared the crap out of him. I had most of what would be my half, minus five thousand dollars. I knew he had the money. I knew I could pay him back in less than a season.

The truth finally surfaced. He wouldn't have any part of it, which left me in his home, on his boat, in his world. I was never going to be a part of his world in the way that served me, too.

In actuality, I didn't need him to follow my dream. We fought on this point. My stance got a little wider and my eyes narrowed. "Fine," I said, "I don't need you for this. I will get a boat of my own."

He immediately snapped, "You will never own a boat of your own."

Game on.

"Really?" Followed by, "Watch me."

Here we go again. Yet another man standing in front of me telling me I am unworthy. What I can and cannot do is between me and my higher self, and nobody else. Here is a little hint to anyone in my future: don't ever tell me I can't. If it is my dream, I will accomplish it, and I look to those with negativity to step aside or get run over.

We broke up and I got my own boat.

I refit her, and then I got a cat. Her name was Sailor.

My sailboat, Sweet P, was simply one of the most learned experiences in my life. I bled, I cried, I panicked, and persevered onboard that boat. I lived aboard and anchored out on the bay side of mile marker 82.5, just off Lorilei's bar and restaurant in Islamorada in the Florida Keys.

Sailing offshore on Charis "His boat"

Sweet P - My boat my home

My Reiki Master Teacher In Sedona, Arizona for my final attunement

Private Chef Job in the Caribbean

Some friends helped me sail her down from Stuart, Florida. We had to go in on high tide because Sweet P, a Union 36, has a six foot draft, which makes it difficult in shallow water but great for offshore.

The anchorage wasn't crowded and I was near to friends that had told me about this little gem of a hide out. I had my car moved down, which would make it easier for trips and evacuations if necessary.

It was necessary. Sailor and I sat out four hurricane evacuations that season in 2004, not to mention a few tropical storms, like Bonnie and Earl. I buddied up with boat neighbors using my car to pack three adults, a cat and a Macaw. That would be Charley, Frances Ivan and Jeanne.

Soon, it would be time to make a change. While living in the Florida Keys, one of those hurricanes put me at a crossroads. It was there that I experienced a visitation.

This was a well-protected anchorage. Aside from the drunks that would try to board my boat bringing me sacks of melted ice in the middle of the night, it was pretty chill. The water was crystal clear and just warm enough for swimming. Not like the Caribbean, but it was close as I could get at the time.

Listening to dolphins blow air next to the hull of the boat was amazing. I watched lobster crawl under my boat. A few of those made it onto the grill. I did not catch them, but I did assist. Life was simple, yet complicated. The ease of the sunsets and warm weather, mixed with the complication of things breaking down was a life that I enjoyed. It's a boat. Everything breaks on a boat, sooner or later. I remember the first thing I ever fixed on my boat was the head, a.k.a. toilet. Of course it would be the shitter that broke first.

There is a sense of freedom when you live aboard a boat. It's a little wild west, and sometimes more adventure than you may bargain for, but it's freedom. I miss that at times. The sound of the water hugging the body of the hull and the gentle breeze skimming your warm skin. As you settle in with a book and a rum drink, contemplating the many stages of the sunset. Or the freedom of simply sipping your first cup of coffee in the morning before the rest of the world starts its chatter. I have to say, I prefer conversations with the dolphin and other sea creatures to what sometimes meets me in a day.

I do not, however, miss the mosquito attacks in the middle of the night, when the wind stops. That incessant buzzing and waiting for the feel of the miniature legs landing on my body, followed by the puncture of a sword into my bloodstream. I smashed more mosquitos on the overhead cabin panel than I care to remember. I should have just painted it red and said be done with it.

While living aboard I took a part-time job at a well-known bathing suit shop called The Lions Den. For reasons written previously, I did not use an outboard on my Fatty Knees dinghy. I rowed everywhere, in all kinds of weather. I rowed to work in the morning and home at night. I did love rowing that dinghy. It was pretty, and I stayed dry for work.

I was doing well at the shop. They trusted me, and I worked hard for the owner. She employed a few people, including her family. I was put in charge of opening alone some days, and that was ok with me. They had video cameras to catch everything.

One morning I opened the shop and my first customer came in about nine or ten. Energetically speaking, this person felt different. She was a she, but she wasn't. She was not male or female. She was not transgender like we would think, because that is our only other choice.

She was not from here. I did not know this until much later.

I chatted with her as she tried on everything. I am here to tell you: everything fit her to perfection no matter what size it was. It morphed on her. It was the craziest thing I had ever seen.

She was gentle and kind when speaking to me. She started talking to me about what I am doing in my life and what's next. I told her about my near death experience. She told me that I was here to give back, and that my path needed to change, that there is a purpose to my life.

We talked for hours as she stacked her items on the counter. She spent over eight hundred dollars in that brief moment in time. Not once did another person enter the store that day, at least while she was there. Not one. This was not normal, but there was nothing normal about that day.

I went home that night thinking of everything we talked about. I kept thinking, "What happened in that shop? And who or what was that Being that came into my life today?"

As if it wasn't strange enough the first time, it happened again the next day. She came back and did the exact same thing. She reiterated that I needed a path change, and what was I doing?

We chatted for hours again, and then she spent another fat wad of cash and floated out the door. Her job was done.

It took two days for the light bulb in my head to start firing off. This was an angelic being, and I couldn't explain it or tell it, as it was, to another living being because they would think I'm nuts. So what did I do with that? I sat with it. I kept it to myself for a long while.

Then, God put my ass right in the middle of a shit-storm hurricane season that shoved sea water up the intake of my Perkins 4108 diesel engine. This forced a haul out and rebuild of the engine.

Meanwhile, I had a good long think about what to do next. Had I had enough? Why was I going through this do-over again? I was 40 yrs old, and in my heart I knew it was time to think about what my visitor had told me. It took me some time, but while searching online about options, I saw an ad for Steiner College in Pompano Beach. They had an associates degree program. I could go back to school and complete a dream I had of getting a degree. There were choices like Massage Therapy, Esthetician, etcetera.

I drove to Pompano Beach to check it out and at least talk to someone about how a person like me could get into the program. As I was touring around the campus, the admin lady kind of sized me up and asked me, "Why are you considering massage school?"

Without even thinking, I said "It's time to give back."

As those words poured out of my mouth, I realized it was December seventeenth, the anniversary date of my near-death experience.

It doesn't become any more clear than that. I packed what little stuff I had in my car, and Sailor and I found a small apartment in Sailboat Bend, Florida, close to the water and not so far from school. I put my boat up for sale and settled back into land life again.

The year was 2005 and I was in south Florida. I thought the previous hurricane season was bad, but 2005 brought more tragedy than anyone could expect. This was the year of Katrina. I had friends that barely dodged that bullet. Their boats didn't fare as well.

A record fifteen hurricanes formed in the 2005 season, and seven of those reached major hurricane status (Category 3 or stronger on the Saffir-Simpson Hurricane Wind Scale). The previous record was twelve hurricanes in the 1969 season.

Many lives were lost. Living where I lived, hurricane Rita breezed by from the East, and then Wilma sucker-punched us from the West. Forecasters said it wasn't going to be more than a Category 1, however as it hit the Everglades and its warm water, the storm increased in power.

Wilma took my roof, but she didn't take my life. I went several weeks without power. I had prepped, but I started running out of gas while charging my phone during the day.

I had to make a break for it. I didn't know how far north I could get before I could get gas. There were stories of horror, loss, and long lines for gas. I made my way out of my neighborhood, driving by the massive upended city block-sized banyan trees, their roots hanging out like the guts of a tortured soldier at war. I didn't realize the pain in my gut was from every living thing dying its slow death all around me. I drove north until I could get gas, then went west to stay with friends in Tampa. When the school got power back I went back home.

The agony of Gaia's pain held me, but at the time I didn't know what was causing me to be so emotional. My day back to school was torturous, and it became worse as I drove home. Everything was still twisted and mangled along the roadside on the highway. Tall signs were gnarled and torn. Trash and pieces of people's lives were splayed out for the world to see.

Out of nowhere, I felt panic. Tears rolled and I couldn't explain where they came from, or why I was feeling this way. I couldn't breathe.

I reached out to my Reiki Master, my teacher and mentor in this new life I had opened up, and she was there for me. She performed a Reiki treatment on me and calmed me down.

I had opened a door into the world of being an empath. I felt everything. If you hurt, I hurt. If you cried, I cried for you, and so on.

This was new to me, but I was learning as fast as I could. While going to massage school I started learning about the mystical world of Spirit, and how to communicate. I investigated near death experience (NDE) and healing groups. I learned about crystals and chakras and all kinds of crazy shit. It was a new path. I read everything I could get my hands on, and then some.

It was not the first I had heard of spirit communications, because I had been to readers before. My introduction to my Reiki Master was a little off the wall, and yet, so memorable.

Side Step....Glass Bubbles

Many years ago, I was living in Rhode Island and working for the award-winning Mad Hatter Bakery at 64 Broadway street. Don't get too excited. I was more of a grunt worker or basic baker.

The owner of the shop, Audra Lalli, is truly an artist. We became good friends. Every now and then, we would wander on over to the Cape for some girl time. This usually included getting a psychic reading at a tiny little bookstore. I can't remember the name of the bookstore, but the reader's name was Sharon.

Sharon was very nice, but her little room was dressed up old school: candles, incense, and it was dark and kinda creepy. She wasn't creepy, but I never understood the whole dark room thing. She would go into a trance and give whatever message she got.

She was very accurate. The thing about psychic readings is, there is no timeline. So you may get a message about something that won't happen for years, and then suddenly you remember how the message connects. Every reader is different. That's why it's always good to record your reading to listen back as many times as you need.

On one occasion, I was given a message about blown glass. Sharon said that one day, I will find myself in a place with blown glass bubbles, and when I am there I will feel as if I'm home.

Well now, this was a mystery. However, remember, there is no timeline with spirit. So I saved the recording for a long time.

Many years passed, with lots of traveling and moving around and life happening, as it does. I found myself making a lane change in life. I went back to school for an associates degree, and became a massage therapist. This was a major crossroads and I was in search of all things astute.

During this whole crossroads time, I went to one of those earthy crunchy New Age events where you can buy readings and crystals and healthy stuff. You can sit in seminars listening to how Angel Therapy works, how we are all energy, etcetera.

I sat in on a few speakers and got a photo of my aura. This is cool; if you have never had it done, do it. It was awesome.

I walked by a small booth where Sally Baldwin was doing free fifteen minute readings. She was selling her book Dying To Live Again. I was still searching for as much information as I could find on dying and near death, so I bought the book and sat for a reading. I found it very interesting, but didn't quite understand it all.

I put my name in a raffle box and was told about an open-to-the-public channeling that Sally did in Pompano Beach. I told her I would go, and had intentions of doing just that.

However, massage school was tiring. I think it was all the twenty-year-old kids I had to sit with in class. I'm twice their age, with half the tolerance. I pulled my tired butt off the couch and went to the public channeling anyway, and found it energizing. It was inspiring to see people get messages from loved ones that have passed.

I picked up a flyer there about Reiki classes. Reiki is defined as "Universal Life Force Energy." Technically speaking, it is a Japanese form of stress reduction. It is that, but so much more. I had been told in the past I should be doing Reiki, but I didn't know much about it, so I never followed up.

At the end of the channeling session they had the raffle from the New Age event. It was for cash, which I thought was strange, but whatever.

Sally pulled my name. I had to pick my chin up off the floor. I am not a "lucky" person in that way. In one hand, I had the flyer for the Reiki class, and in the other I was getting ready to accept the check. I told Sally to make the check out to the Reiki Master and whatever is left, give back to the foundation. So she did, and so I did.

It was at that moment that I formally met my Reiki Master Teacher Ellen Joy Pritchard.

Joy teaches Usui Reiki Ryoho. I signed on for the first and second classes. I had no idea what I was getting into, but it was the beginning of my awakening.

A few weeks later the class was at the teacher's house, and an all day event. It was a crystal-clear Florida sunshine day. The front of the house had a tall gate, so you couldn't see the front door from the street.

I stepped through the gate and into a tiny courtyard with beautiful blown glass bubbles hanging from everywhere.

Yeah, don't get too excited. I didn't "get it" at the time. It wasn't until the class sat down to start going over the handbook that uncontrollable tears started pouring out of my eyes. I mean, really, sometimes I just annoy myself when that happens.

The message and memory came back loud and clear. "When you find yourself surrounded by blown glass bubbles it will be like coming home." Sharon the psychic was right.

Once I explained to everyone what I was blubbering about, we carried on with the class. It was that day that I turned a corner and opened myself up completely to the healing arts and focused more on giving back. It is why I am here.

I recommend my Master Teacher to anyone who is looking to become attuned to Reiki. I also advise that once you have started with a Master Teacher, stick with that same person if you plan on pursuing higher levels of learning with Reiki.

Below are the Reiki ideals as presented by Mrs. Hawayo Takata. She is the one who brought Reiki to the West. For this, I stand in gratitude.

The Reiki Ideals

Just for today, I will let go of anger.

Just for today, I will let go of worry.

Just for today, I will give my thanks for my many blessings.

Just for today, I will do my work honestly.

Just for today , I will be kind to my neighbor and every living thing.

By 2006 I earned my first and only degree an "Associates in Science of Natural Health with a focus on Therapeutic Massage." I went back in the trenches to get that stinking piece of paper. That meant Algebra, my arch nemesis. It gave me flashbacks of falling asleep in class when I was barely fifteen. I got through it, though, and all that crappy math aside, I had discovered how to help people heal by doing massage and Reiki.

I also learned to channel, or as some would call it, dowsing. I studied under Sally Baldwin. She taught about Angels and Spirit communication using a pendulum and a letter board. This method, as I learned much later in life, means nothing to most mediums in the United Kingdom. We will get to my opinion on that.

I don't know where I got the bright idea to move after graduation. I took the national boards for massage therapy and passed. I could work anywhere. North Carolina was calling my name, and so I packed up and went.

For the first time in my entire moving history, and that's a lot, I hired a moving company to get to Asheville, North Carolina... which I do not recommend, by the way. This company held my furniture hostage, saying they couldn't get the truck into the complex. Fuckers. Of course they lied and charged me more money. Fuckers.

But fresh mountain air would be a nice change, right? It wasn't bad, but I never really fit in. I spoke a different language. There were lots of people that claimed to be so open and spiritual, but really there were only a few like that, Nina the Oracle of Asheville being one of them.

Nina is a phenomenal spirit artist and communicator. If you are ever in Asheville, seek her out; she is amazing.

While in Asheville, I worked at a spa in the village. I never fit in there. Fancy spas were not my thing. My volume was turning up, energetically speaking. I could feel people, and started hearing things about them, and channeling much needed information for them. At the same time, my tolerance for bullshit grew increasingly lower.

Before my move to Asheville, I had received my Master Teacher Attunement for Usui Ryoho Reiki. I could teach, and so I did. I had my very first students In Asheville.

It was scary and fascinating all at the same time. I continually looked in the rear view mirror at where I came from. I think there was a part of me waiting for the rug to be pulled out from under me. Had I really earned my degree? Could I really be a Master Teacher? I had done all of the studies and tests and work that was required of me as a teacher. So yes, I could be all of those things and more. It just hadn't sunk in yet.

While living in Asheville I took a trip of a lifetime to Thailand. I spent a little more than three weeks studying traditional Thai massage and reflexology. It was an amazing experience on so many levels.

Thailand was a third world country pretending to be more. The hotel we were booked into was still putting mattresses into the rooms upon our arrival. I was electrocuted in my bathroom on a daily basis due to bad wiring. I knew what this was because I had experienced the same thing in the Caribbean.

The aroma of fresh jasmine and gardenia wafted from Chiang Mai markets. There were warnings that fruits like Durian were not allowed near the hotel due to their smell. I took the hint and didn't bother even trying it. I didn't want to taste anything that smelled like ass.

In school, we had uniforms to wear and traditions to follow. It was so much to learn packed into a very short time. I experienced receiving Thai massage in Bangkok and Chiang Mai. Bangkok is rough. I didn't care for the roughness of the massage, or the city. The smog was so thick and toxic we were encouraged to wear protective face masks. Traffic in Bangkok stood still and the fumes floated around and soaked into peoples lungs and onto their skin. It was crowded and nasty and offensive, like most big cities. I was happy to arrive in Chiang Mai.

I brought tools for channeling and angel cards for connecting with angels. I did Soul Chart readings for people just about every day after school. I think that is ultimately why I was there.

I sat in temples with the monks. As women, we were warned we could not speak to them or touch them. I averted my eyes until I couldn't.

I went to a temple where I was blinded by the energy of what turned out to be female monks dressed in white. They did speak to people, and shared their joy. They were some of the most angelic beings I've ever seen on earth.

Schooling during the day, channeling in the afternoon, and sipping wine at night, that was how I rolled in Thailand. I experienced a beautiful culture and gorgeous landscapes. Peaceful temples and majestic elephants in jungle surroundings were common on this trip.

When I returned to North Carolina and was informed by the spa owners that Thai massage really wasn't going to fit in their "menu" of treatments, I decided it was time to rethink my place there. God helped me with that decision by putting me in a snowstorm on a mountain highway.

I had assisted my Thai instructor in her class in Charlotte, North Carolina and had to drive home to Asheville. It was not that big of a deal until the snow and ice started. The road went from a four lane mountain highway to barely a two lane highway with a safe top speed of about thirty miles per hour.

By the time I made it back to my apartment, the road was a thick sheet of ice, something me and my Toyota Camry were unprepared for.

I had forgotten the road to the apartment was actually steep. Here is where I had my Florida ass handed to me on a platter. As I was driving and looking at the slope I kept thinking, "Don't stop, just keep it steady, and for god's sake no brakes!"

I made it about half way before my car ignored the gas I was giving it and started sliding sideways.

This is not the direction I intended to go.

I was not alone.

There were others a bit higher up going through the same thing. I let my car slide comfortably to the edge and stopped there. With all my brakes on, I put the car in park and locked the car.

I walked the rest of the snowy hill in my thin Thai massage uniform. Clearly, it was time to move. Definitely. No question, without a doubt.

I do not do snow.

Well, I do not do snow unless I am inside a comfy cottage with a fireplace and plenty of wood to burn, wine to drink and food to eat, and a nice looking man to nibble on. Just sayin, those are my rules.

Soon after that experience, I sold all of my furniture and boxed everything up in no time flat. I loaded a small truck and towed my car and Sailor and I hit the road. Destination: Venice, Florida.

If you have ever lived in Florida, you don't want to do a lot of driving in "love bug" season… which is when I chose to move. My moving truck was slathered in dead love bugs. I'm not talking a few dozen, I'm talking thousands. Little black and red flying insects connected by their juicy parts, only to be met with a kamikaze death when they hit the truck. It's gross, but it is a part of Florida living that I can handle. I would rather experience that than freeze my ass off on a mountain and risk Sailor looking at me like I was a good choice for dinner. Yuck.

Sailor and I arrived unscathed and settled into Venice only a mile from one of the best Florida beach bars, Sharkey's.

I stayed in Venice for a short time. It was another one of those situations where I put the pendulum over the map and let my peeps guide me.

 Not in complete blind faith. I did take a road trip and got a feeling for the area first. I fell in love with the sunsets at the beach in Venice. I felt a sense of peace in that area. I went back to Asheville, got someone to pick up my lease, sold all my shit and moved.

It was a place to be for a while. The median age, unfortunately for me, was 76. Not conducive to a healthy dating life unless I wanted to turn into a "sugar baby," which, of course, was not going to happen. Ewww.

Chapter 11

While living in Venice I received a call from a distraught friend. She had left her husband and needed a place to land. I had the space and time to help. As any of my friends know I will always have the door open in their time of need. It's only when one questions my integrity or lies to me that the door slams shut. Anyway, this friend healed and moved back to her southern roots in Louisiana and I set off to my next destination, Panama.

People ask me how I liked living in Panama. I have to say that I lived there six years, and that was five years too long.

Look where I came from. Look at my history. I have dealt with assholes and idiots most of my life. I have been to many small third world countries and have never experienced anything like the culture of Panama. Or shall I call it what it really is: Manama.

To say that the men radiate machismo is an understatement. The women are just as bad. They lie like they breathe.

I should have known better, but I thought to myself, "I have traveled the world, or a lot of it, anyway, and I can handle this." Nothing could be worse than my roots or lack thereof. I was wrong, so wrong. But when I found myself stuck financially in the jungle community about an hour north of Panama City, it felt like a noose was tightening around my neck.

Now look, I know there is a reason why I was. It didn't become clear to me until much later.

The crash of 2008 financially killed me and so many others. The only saving grace for me was that I was still relatively young. I could still work. Some people could not, and they lost more than their cushion. In some cases, they lost their lives.

I had to choose. I chose to journey on, sell everything I owned and make the move to Panama with Sailor and Jack. The boy kitty was a new addition, and one that Sailor wasn't to happy about. We needed balance and Panama Jack (now "just Jack") was it. In my heart I want to say I regret it, but I have to pay homage to my soul's journey. I had to hit a low I didn't see coming.

I named my guest house in Los Altos de Cerro Azul "Ginger House" after a favorite place of mine in Thailand, and because the property was surrounded by so many different types of wild ginger.

I dedicated some of my limited funds to hire a tech employee who worked for a friend of mine to create my website. I figured he wouldn't cheat me because I was friends with his boss.

Fucker stole my domain name and held it hostage. Liars, cheats, and thieves. It became a new normal in the world that would be my home for six years.

I became friends with Jennifer King, a woman from a gourmet group I joined. She saved my ass on more than one occasion while I was living in that hellhole. I can hear her telling me, "Oh, websites? I can help you with that." I should have listened to her. She was not Panamanian.

Later she created my website for the business and became one of my most logical and frustratingly intelligent besties. I gained a profoundly important person in my life. It kills me how right she is about shit.

Most of the challenges I faced in this primitive place were the result of having to depend on people who were not dependable. It's like having someone else take the helm and then you see they have removed the steering wheel. It's crazy.

The expat community in Cerro Azul was OK. Not great, but OK. Everyone, it seemed, had their own agenda. There were those that secretly didn't want a business like mine in the community. None of the Panamanians that owned property in that area wanted me to have a guest house so it was a constant battle.

I remember all too well when a neighbor in the community who happened to be an attorney filed a complaint with the government that I didn't have a health card. She was right. I didn't have a health card because I wasn't told I needed one. So the police showed up one day.

This was not good, because anything could happen when the police showed up at your door. He came with a paper that showed I could be closed down, that I had to get a health card, and blah blah blah.

There was a small, very primitive clinic on the mountain. This is where the people came that lived in hidden villages in the jungle. I was told to get there and get in line hours before opening. Getting this health card would consist of a full day of tests and talks and dismissive attitudes because of my color and nationality.

I got in line at 4:30 in the morning. It was still dark when I walked up to the clinic, and I could hear the wildlife sussing us out as we waited for the doors to open. I wasn't the first in line that day -- I think I was 3rd.

I went in when I was called for my turn, which should have been after the second person in line but of course wasn't.

I call that "walking while white." Racism in Panama does exist, and not quietly. It's big and bold and very much in your face.

My heart was checked, my weight was checked, and I waited. I was made to sit in a dental chair… yes, they checked my teeth so I could operate a guest house. As I sat waiting in the chair to have my teeth checked, flies buzzed around, landing on everything.

Oh yes, but wait, it gets better. After my teeth were poked at, I was told to wait in another room so that a woman could come and have a charla (chat) with me.

 Eventually this little old lady came in and started talking about God and my relationship with the Lord. This is something you need to go through in order to obtain a health card in Panama. You must be right with the Lord to run a guest house in Panama.

But wait, it gets even better than that. My last and final test that day was to be conducted by the very man in charge that came to my property that day with the paper and the fine. He sat in front of me and told me that there would have to be an "examination."

Ladies, you know what I mean.

This was my line. Talk to me about God all you want; poke a little at my teeth and gums, but fuck you if you think I am spreading my legs for your filthy little face to crawl up in there. Hell to the no.

Things got a little loud. It was well into the day and I had already been there 12 hours. At the top of my lungs, I said, "You want to look in my vagina? Why is it that you want to look into my vagina? Are you a Gynecologist?"

This went on and the quieter he got, the louder I got. I leaned over to grab my ID from his clipboard and he grabbed it at the same time.

A direct challenge to me.

I looked this asshole in the eye and said, "No way are you going to touch me or look at my vagina. Ever."

I know he could feel my rage because I aimed it right at his core. We tugged back and forth with the photo until finally he gave in and gave me the piece of paper I needed.

All this because a Panamanian businesswoman did not want me to have paying guests stay at my home. This is how they operate there. It was the same woman that later made a fake report to the police that I had guns in my home.

That was a fun day. It went like this:

One quiet, drizzling day during the rainy season, I heard cars racing down the jungle road. I lived at the end of my road and there was usually no traffic... except when things like this happened. I jumped up and ran to the window to see what or who was driving into my yard.

Two Policia trucks pulled in and out poured about six men in full SWAT gear.

The first thing I did was yell at them to back their trucks off of my grass.

They marched up, speaking Spanish at me, guns drawn. I learned never to speak Spanish, or try to speak Spanish, in situations like this. I'm glad I listened to that advice, because I think it saved me on more than one occasion.

They asked me about my guns. I said, "I don't understand."

Finally, two officers who spoke English, a woman and man, said there had been a report that I had illegal guns in my home.

I laughed.

They did not.

I informed them I was there alone except for two cats, I didn't own any guns, and guns were not allowed in my home.

They were going to search my home whether I liked it or not. I stood there solo, in a foreign country, and said, "Fine, but you are going to remove your boots."

And they did! It was the only way that I could disarm them.

Only two of the six came in. They tore through everything in my home, scoping out every nook and cranny and lifting everything that wasn't nailed down

They had been duped. After I stopped shaking, I had to laugh. This kind of trouble found its way to me because I am not one to simply take another person's shit. Some of the expats may have said I brought it on myself. Well, fuck you and the horse you rode in on. I had enough abuse in my life, and wasn't going to let more just happen to me; not without a fight.

Example: El Machetazo, a very local grocery store in the town of 24 de Diciembre just down the mountain from where I lived, was always a challenge. It's guarded by men armed with assault rifles. The locals stared at me, or gave dirty looks. It was my new normal.

I remember standing in a long line in the vegetable section of the store to get my veggies weighed and priced as required by the store. I noticed a very tall and very fat pregnant woman standing toward the front. She was not in line, and she was not going to get in line. She was waiting. A few more people ahead of me had their items weighed and priced, and then came my turn.

The pregnant beast stepped in front of me. I said, "Excuse me, but the line is back there."

She turned and fired back that this was her country, and that she was pregnant, and if I didn't like it, to get out of her country; I didn't belong here anyway.

I stopped her there. I said, "It's not my fault you're pregnant; everyone in Panama is pregnant, but the line starts back there."

Everyone behind me looked either down or away. I had done it now. I had poked the dragon.

Inside, I was cracking up laughing. I had come to the crossroads of I Don't Give a Shit Street and Who Cares Lane. I was over being pushed around because of my color and nationality. Plenty of Panamanians were in my country and never saw me jumping the line or pushing them around.

Well, the person weighing things grabbed the woman's stuff and, with unprecedented rapid-fire speed, weighed her stuff and handed it off. She continued to blast me even as she walked away.

I looked behind me and waited for someone to say something. There I was, walking while white again.

I needed confirmation. Apparently, it is a law that anyone who is old or pregnant has the right to jump any line they see fit. I have, on many occasions, let elders in front of me without even blinking an eye. I have never witnessed a pregnant woman jump the line in front of her own country's people. This one did it to me because I was a white woman walking in her country.

As I live and breathe, I will never treat people the way I was treated in Panama.

Side Step….A Primitive Place

Coming to be in this place, this jungle, in Central America, has guided me in a way I'd never considered before. I can be so hard headed at times, I'm not surprised it took coming to such a remote place to get some self-realization.

For so long now, I've seen myself as stuck here and unable to make a move in any direction. There is, of course, a reason I'm here so long. It's not to be closer to people I thought were my friends, and it's not because I'm actually stuck. I'm simply moving through some stuff at a glacial pace.

I'm writing this sitting at the edge of a cascada, a waterfall. It's a primitive part of Panama, surrounded by elementals, nature's little spirit friends.

The waterfall is fast and furious, like my emotions. It's powerful like my heart. It's soft in its edges as it mists up into the air after coming into contact with rough rocks weathered by centuries of pounding storms. There are small areas where it gathers and calms itself before moving forward, tumbling down the mountain in all of its glory.

Astrologically, I am a Leo, which is a fire sign. I have always turned to water to balance me.

In the last day or so, I've been dreaming of my next place, and the twin flame that will embrace me there, but I'm still coming to grips with the scarring on my face. You might not think after all of these years that it would still be an issue. It is for me. Every day I look in the mirror, I see the misshapen eye and the vertical scar that runs the length of my face.

I question myself in crowds of people. Who is noticing, and who isn't? I didn't realize I was hiding behind a tough exterior so I wasn't vulnerable to rejection. I've worked very hard at protecting myself, all the while pushing away chances at love. As I grow and change I realized up until recently I've been rejecting men before they even had a chance to see me, the real me.

I know in my heart I'm a good person with many gifts. I hadn't understood that keeping those gifts to myself is one of the most non-astute things I could ever do. If someone like me was sitting in front of me, I would say to her, "You are not just the physical body we all know. You are loving energy, as well."

I would say to her, "You are first a soul, then a human, and lastly a woman. So the importance of having a scar-free face isn't really so important after all. If you can see this, then so can everyone else. Being a woman in this society, where beauty is the focus, it makes it so difficult to be authentic."

Simply saying these words makes it seem so easy, but it's not. This is me giving it my best try. I don't want to keep my gifts to myself anymore. I want to share with people who can see through that heavy veil of protection I've put over me until I'm ready to shed it completely.

I don't have to sail around the world or climb the highest mountain. I'm strong, but I don't have to be stronger or more fierce to gain the admiration of those around me. I can just be the beautiful soul that I am. No matter what, I will always be that soul first, and everything else will follow and be as it should be. Anchored in love.

Some people may say, "How could it be all bad in Panama?"

To that, I would say, "OK, maybe it wasn't all bad, but the parts that were good were not from Panama. The good parts were my guests that came from all over the world. There were bird watchers (twitchers & tweekers), photographers, and writers.

One of my favorite guests was a photographer from the Czech Republic by the name of Petr Bambousek.

It was around sunset, and I was standing at the kitchen sink facing the patio preparing dinner. Petr walked up and said, "Hey Picasso, check this out."

I shut off the running water, dried my hands, and leaned over to see what was on his camera screen. It was a picture of a hummingbird, which was beautiful in and of itself, but this tiny little bird had the reflection of the sunset in its eye.

That shot was one in a million. It will be forever embedded in my memory as one of the greats. Moments of that caliber kept me breathing when I didn't want to any more.

Many of my guests were people from the United States looking for another place to be, or a retirement place that wouldn't drain their bank accounts and shove pharmaceuticals down their throats. While the latter is true, the former was not. Panama loves American money, it just doesn't love the American people. There is still a big fat chip on their shoulder from the days of former dictator Manuel Noriega, when the United States came storming in and shot up the town.

Unfortunately, these would-be expatriates had been soaking up the lies printed in International Living for years. I guess because they read it in a magazine or saw it on a real estate reality show they expected it would be true.

It was not, and oftentimes I saw people come into the country and try to settle down only to become victims of either a real estate scam or property fraud. It was an awful, shameful, horrific thing to watch these senior citizens who had just been stolen from in the crash of

2008 look for solace in another land, only to be cheated out of their hard-earned money yet again.

Most of the world has this incredible idea that Americans are all filthy rich Hollywood millionaires. Their image of us is based on what they see on TV or at the movies.

They don't know about our hungry and jobless people. Nobody ever tells them that in our promised land, there are thousands of people walking around just a few bucks away from complete destitution. We have farms and factories that have shut down for lack of money. There are people like me that didn't have opportunities because I kept falling through the cracks.

People like me are invisible to the rest of the world. The world is not shown, or doesn't want to see, what is really happening in our country. We are not rich. Only one percent of the population has money. The rest of us are struggling to keep our heads above water. It's a sad thing. What they see is make believe, and yet they believe.

There was a time or two when I had to come out of my home in the middle of the jungle with a machete in my hand because someone thought they could get to me. This was a serious error in judgement on their part.

For example, one night, near the end of my time in Panama, a man tried to crawl through my guest's bedroom window. I was awoken by the gentleman of the couple saying, "Picasso, there is a man trying to climb through the window. He opened our screen and said in Spanish he was looking for the lady in the green car."

That would be me. That fucker.

I told my guest to stay inside, quickly grabbed a machete and my flashlight, and went running out of the house screaming, "Come and get me, you motherfucker! You want me, I'm right fucking here! Come on out, you rat bastard chicken shit! I'm ready for you, you piece of shit!"

There was a street light at the end of my road and another farther down, but that was it. I don't know where that guy went, but he never came back.

The next day, I went to the police and told them someone better find that guy, because if they don't and I do, I'm gonna kill him. This would be on them. I gave fair warning that if it's between me and him, there is gonna be a fight and someone is gonna disappear. It wasn't gonna be me.

Every ounce of bottled-up rage from being raped and molested and abused in my past came gurgling up. I had that in me, and I could pull from when I needed it. Just step in my swirl of rage and see what happens.

I was up for the challenge. I set traps around my windows so I could get footprints that were not mine. I have never thought of myself as one who could take a life, but in that state of mind I believed in my heart that it was possible. I had found my line in the sand and no mother-fucking dick-swinging Panamanian asshole was going to touch me.

Ever.

It took me quite a long time to calm down from that incident. I was encouraged to start writing as a way to cope. The blog would come to be my training wheels. There, I wrote out the anger, fear and hurt that had enveloped my entire being. I had a lot to pull from when it came to emotional experiences. Writing seemed to bring so much stuff to the surface.

Side Step....Begin Again

It was on this date nineteen years ago that I did exactly that. I began again. My life had been taken from me by an outboard motor; my face slashed; my body, broken. My already low self-esteem instantly got lower. There were so many different levels of who I was before I died, but none were apparent to me until I went and came back. Even then, it took a while to realize I am powerful enough to stay if I want to. I am worthy of being here and making my presence known.

I may speak a different language than most. I may interpret what you say to me in a way you didn't expect. It's who I am. I chose to be a woman in this life, and I chose to be short. I am powerful, so if you can imagine me a foot taller with all of that power and energy, I would literally scare the shit out of people.

We don't want that, now, do we?

When the propeller went through my face and sliced the nerves that control my smile, it killed me in a different, much more intense way.

There was so much healing to be done. I had to heal not

just from my death, but also from my life before my death.

Dying is the easy part, and oh, so beautiful. If I could give you a word to describe what I felt… the word would be "peace."

Loving, unconditional peace filled my soul. I felt protected, and yet, there was nothing to be protected from, because there was nothing to fear in death.

I honor the life I had before my death, because it gave me the experiences that enable me to help others today. I can sit in front of you and say, "Nothing is perfect, and yet everything is perfect, and as it should be."

We all have those lessons that help mold us. Some of us have a few more than others because we don't always get it the first time around.

Today, I stand before you as a strong, beautiful spirit. I am confident and loving. I am creative, smart, and worldly. I am able and willing to help you up if you are feeling down. I will slay the damn dragon if you ask me. Just ask me.

It's not every day I feel this way, but because it is the day it is, I am honoring how far I have come. I am honoring my ability to pull from the core of my soul's journey, and from all of my experiences. My body was slashed and torn, and then I was judged by my peers, by the law, by the community, and by those who might employ me.

To judge me is not to know me.

If you knew where I came from and what I had been through, there would be no judgement, only honor and appreciation. I survived all of the above to be here, in the moment, so I can learn to love myself. It's the hardest thing in the world to do, and nothing I was ever taught over the years, but I'm going to learn to make this second nature in my heart. I am learning to love and appreciate my strength and knowing.

Nineteen years ago, I was living a dream of sailing and working on the water, being one with the sea, and earning my props. Then the channel changed and I got a do-over.

Living the dream didn't change. I went through thirteen surgeries and lots of pain, but I kept sailing and communing with the sea. I continued because I wasn't going to let anyone tell me I didn't belong or that I couldn't do what I was doing.

I am a warrior soul who has always embraced challenges; it's what I do best. I get things done and fight for the underdog. Well, in my case I was the underdog, so I fought for myself. My intent today was to go to battle, but instead I chose a different path. A battle still, but not on the outside. It's a battle on the inside, and the only one that gets in my way now and again.

As I usually do, today I opened my heart to channeling. Today I chose to listen, to live in a way that's higher in vibration and higher in love. My hope is that you feel and hear my words and compare them to your own journey.

That is why I am here. I am a warrior soul who was too tough to kill, and now am here to be of service to those of you who choose to reach out. I not only honor myself in my words today, but I honor you as well. Love and light to those of you who choose to read what I have to offer.

Writing the This Seekers Journey blog became a healthy distraction. It helped me start the process of healing old wounds. Even though I thought I had accomplished that task through countless hours of therapy and Adult Children of Alcoholics meetings, I was nowhere near being right or balanced.

As an empath, I am affected by loud things: loud voices, loud music, and nonsensical gibberish coming from religious fanatics with microphones… all of which I experienced in Panama.

Panamanians would come from the city to their weekend homes in a mountain community called Altos de Cerro Azul and blast music twenty four hours a day from the time they arrived to the time they drove off the mountain.

Of course, the jungle is very noisy itself, but it's a natural noise that can be pleasing to the ears; the sound of crickets, cicadas, and the howler monkeys that sat in the trees at the edge of the property peering at me and wondering what the hell I was doing in their jungle.

I can tell you, howlers, I'm still not sure why I was there.

The noise from the natives was at one volume and one volume only: unbearable. One day, I had enough of the blasted pounding from a swimming pool community clubhouse hosting a fancy party.

I was looking rough that day. I had a massive headache, and no sleep thanks to the weekend parties. I drove to the pool, but the gate was closed and guarded by security.

That didn't stop me. I was on a mission. I'm sure I looked like I broke out of an insane asylum.

I ran onto the bandstand and screamed at them to turn that shit down. The dancers stopped and looked at me like I was crazy. I was crazy. I was crazy mad.

I yelled at the top of my lungs that it had to stop, that they were shaking my windows with their offensive thumping senseless noise. I threatened to start cutting wires.

I was that close to the edge with these people. Lucky for them, I forgot my machete.

I left their stage after saying my peace. I'm sure it was talked about how the crazy gringa went off her rocker. I didn't care.

Did they stop, or turn down the music?

Of course not.

Los Altos de Cerro Azul is a gated community situated in the Chagres National Park in Panama. Imagine what that sort of vibration does to animals trying to find food or the way back to their nests.

It is not a country of caring people. It is simple as that. The Panamanian people care only about themselves.

Period.

Side Step….I Belong

This is for those who have tried in the past and who are trying now to make me disappear.

Does your noise offend me?

Do your lies erode me?

Yes, I feel you trying to chip away

At my very Soul, my very Being

You fear me, I see

You loath my voice of reason

Because you know not what reason is

You do not claim responsibility in your badness

Yet you create more badness everyday

Where is your conscience?

Your sense of right and wrong

All I hear is go away, you don't belong

You press your loudness into my brain

It hurts so much it drives me insane

Your ego leads you to create more

More drama and lies, like your keeping score

High points for pain and damage along the way

I see it clearly everyday

You want to shut me up, so I'll go away

My memory is long and my voice runs true

I'll call you out on your lies when I'm through

Yes your noise offends me and your lies baffle me

But you will never erode my Being, my Soul

So step aside or move along

I am here, I belong

Chapter 12

Even as things began to get more difficult in Panama, I was losing the important, delicate connection between me and my mom back in the States. There were moments I was trying to regain with mom and over the years I kept failing.

She was on her third husband, and as much as I tried, there was no bonding with him. For my mom, though, that man was her world. It would be the same, and worse, as she advanced into her golden years. Her world rotated around the man in her life.

I wanted so much to have a "normal" relationship with my mom. There had been so much healing from old anger and hurt, it seemed like maybe good things could begin to happen. So the question now was, could there be hope for a beautiful mother-daughter experience at the end?

The answer to that was a definite no. Just when I thought maybe we could have that as adults, life took yet another unexpected turn.

In 2008, before my move to Panama, I was guilted into going to a family reunion in Southern California. I wanted nothing to do with this trip, but I struck up a deal with my mom. In my forty-something years on this planet, she had only ever come to my home on two occasions. I had always gone to her. So she agreed to visit me in Florida, where we would then travel together to California for the reunion.

It was on this visit that she admitted she was a little scared she was losing her memory. She was forgetting things she wouldn't normally forget.

I said, "Let's keep track of this and get you in to see someone."

She agreed, and this was the last I heard of it.

On that trip I realized mom was losing her ability to hold on to things in her mind. I'm sure it was terrifying to her to say the least.

Needless to say, the family reunion was filled with drama and swirls of things that I no longer wanted or had the tolerance for in my life. My mother had six kids, total. I was the only one who didn't live in California, and I was the only one to show up for her.

It was sad. But she created that mess, unfortunate as it is. She was raised up in poverty and pain and abuse, and ran from it. There were no real roots for her.

She eventually re-connected with her siblings, but in her mind reality played out differently. She thought she was the leader of the family. If you ask her surviving brothers and sisters, I'm sure you will get a different story.

We moved so many times, there was never a chance for stability. Nobody showed her how to create a bond with her children, and I can't fault her for that. It is what she learned and what she created from what she learned.

Sadly in her most important declining years, the only family member who showed up to represent her part of the family was a bastard child that looked exactly like her.

In addition to all of the family drama, one of the worst things that happened on that trip was the loss of a twenty year-plus friendship.

I had been dissed again by my best friend (at the time) so she could get laid by a fling she had met on vacation a few months earlier. There are certain things you do not do to your friends. So I chose to step away from a friend with whom I had been through everything.

You do not dis your friends for a dude, anytime, ever. I needed a friend at that time, dealing with what I was dealing with, and she chose not to be present.

It hurt to the core. I didn't belong in that state, or with that family, or in that friendship. All arrows pointed south and east to Panama. So off I went.

In the six years I lived in Panama, I never felt like it was home. It was prickly and uncomfortable and, quite honestly, I almost didn't make it out alive. Money was very scarce when there weren't guests. At one point I sold my personal upstairs bedroom set and lived downstairs in the guest rooms.

I remember a time in the last year of my stay, when I had $2.69 to my name. My cats Sailor and Jack had food, however I did not. My body started shutting down. Being in a constant state of fight or flight was taking a physical toll on me, and all I could think about was how I couldn't get back to my mom to protect her at this time in her life.

Side Step….Dear Mom…

It's almost two in the morning and I can't sleep because I'm thinking about you and me. This is the time when I would like to say thanks so much for being such a wonderful mom and being so supportive through the years, but I can't. I want to say, more than anything, that I want to be there for you in this time of need, not for who you were then, but who you are now.

We have never had that loving mother-daughter relationship. It's been rocky for so many years. I remember never being able to buy you a normal mother's day card without it being an absolute lie.

You were the one who told me never ever fall in love. I can still hear you say it to this day. I was young and wanted nothing more than to do just that.

You taught me to fight for the underdog, but somehow I learned to fight for everything because I had no choice.

When I was young and there was something I wanted, you told me, "Wish in one hand and shit in the other and see which one gets full fastest."

Each time you ran away from home I feared I would never see you again, so when you took me with you on occasion in the middle of the night, I cherished it being just you and me, even though you were drunk, because I loved you so much.

You kicked me out of the house when I was fourteen, then told me I was a stupid child. I cried so hard I couldn't breathe for days. Years later, in some crazy stupor, you sent me a silly little refrigerator magnet that said, "Don't Quit." I was nineteen. I'm now forty-eight, and I still have it.

Well mom, I am here to say I didn't quit. I'm still here, and after all of the crap and craziness you brought to my life, and I to yours, I still love you with all of my heart. I want so much to be there for you, and I hope that I get the chance.

When I was very little, you loved me. I know you did. I came from a relationship of love. He wasn't your husband, but he was your best friend and soulmate. There, I will say, you did something very right and out of love.

You shared this secret with me when I was eight years old. It was the hardest thing in the world to be that age and know I didn't belong to the family the way everyone else did. You should have let me share that secret. That's OK, because I have shared it now.

That man who was my father would cry tears from heaven for you if he could. He loved you so much.

Over the years, as you and I are aging women we have bonded in better ways. We have shared our passion for food. You taught me how to take care of guests in my home, and now look at me, mom, I run a guest house.

I tried to absorb as much love from you as I possibly could. As much as you were able to give me, anyway. Before you go, I want to laugh with you so hard that we pee just a little. I want to feed you some of the recipes I've learned on my own, and have us taste some of the old tried-and-true ones once again.

I want us to walk on fall days and look at the colors you are so fond of while I hold your arm so close to me. I want to sit by the fire and listen to some old stories about your rebellious teen years. I want to make a bunch of tapas and open a bottle of wine, pile up on the couch, and watch a good movie. I know that we are moving on to the next stages of our lives but please, please don't push me away now. Let me be there for you, and I will take what you can give me and accept it.

You can be pretty damn mean, but I want to love you so much that it softens the edges of your hard heart. Let me be the daughter I have always wanted to be.

This is what I'm thinking of at two in the morning. It's keeping me awake. I will sip my sleepy-time tea, go back to bed, and hopefully dream of love and laughter, because I've had enough sorrow and heartbreak.

I won't quit, though, mom, I won't give up hoping there is a little spark in you that's left for me.

I love you mom.

Don't Quit

When things go wrong, as they sometimes will

When the road you're trudging seems all uphill

When the funds are low and the debts are high

And you want to smile but you have to sigh

When care is pressing you down a bit

Rest if you must but don't you quit

Life is queer with its twists and turns

As everyone of us sometimes learns

And many a person turns about

When they might have won, had they stuck it out

Don't give up though the pace seems slow

You may succeed with another blow

Often the struggler has given up

When he might have captured the victor's cup

And he learned too late when the night came down

How close he was to the golden crown

Success is failure turned inside out

So stick to the fight when you're hardest hit

It's when things seem worse when you mustn't quit.

~ John Greenleaf Whittier

In Panama, I would watch wildlife as a form of entertainment. The Capuchin monkeys would stand on branches and shake them to see if I would react. The mono titi (Geoffroy tamarin) were sweet and gentle, often coming around asking for bananas. Then I started seeing more snakes on the property, and I knew change was coming.

I tried to make conversation with my mom on Skype, but she could no longer operate the computer I bought her.

Or the phone.

I knew things were bad when she started talking to me about me. That's when my heart sunk.

I was thousands of miles away and I had no control over when the house sold or when I could leave. So I read everything I could get a hold of about Alzheimer's. I set up home checks to make sure mom was safe, since her husband insisted on working and leaving her home alone with a gas stove and a fireplace.

I tried to stress the importance of him being around to make sure she didn't wander off or burn the house down. They had already gone through that once. She certainly could not survive that again.

Before my move to Panama, and not long after the family reunion, my mom lost a sister to cancer. Then, their house, the oldest in the community, built in 1809, burned to the ground. The final straw was she broke her hip when she fell in the basement... while home alone.

I believe the anesthesia from the surgery and the grief from the loss of her sister propelled her into a state of Alzheimer's that she could never return from.

I was an illegal alien the last two years I lived in Panama. I couldn't afford to cross the border and get my passport stamped. I could barely afford food. This also meant I couldn't make the loan payment on the house.

I eventually found a buyer for the house but he and his wife were absolute fucking idiots. He bragged that he was the first Zonian (a person living in the Panama Canal Zone) to get a passport under Noriega. Great claim to fame, dude.

Things were muddled with complications, mostly because that is how Panama is no matter what you are doing. Accomplishing anything takes a stack of stamps on each document.

Side Step....9 Stamps

Panama is sucking the life out of me. I have no idea how I have made it this long, living here. It was only going to be for a few years, and then things got way off track. There is no logic in this country and no compassion. It feels soulless, cold and uncaring. Yet I am still here, gutting it out.

I stand waiting for clerks and judges and attorneys to do what they say they are going to do. Mostly they say this or that will happen, and of course it doesn't. Am I surprised? No, but I am exhausted by the lies and the unnecessary bureaucracy.

I'm calling this story "9 Stamps" because of the most recent document that took three attorneys, a judge, and a bank to push through the system (yet it's still not complete). On this document there are nine stamps and eight signatures. This is one document, and it took over a month to get to the end... only to be told it will be another forty-five days before it's over.

In the meantime, I find it hard to breathe, and even harder to believe I am putting up with the inhumanity of it all. It started by me defaulting on a loan (not on purpose) due to the ever-increasing cost of living here in Panama (where it's supposed to be more affordable... unless you are white and not from here). Yet I kept going on with the business and trying to communicate with the bank involved. I would call and try to speak to them in their language, and they would hang up. I would call back... and they would hang up.

The bank was taken over by another bank, and there was, of course, no notification of this happening. I tried to call again. Same thing, I call and they hang up.

In the meantime I was trying to sell my home due to the fact that my mother was diagnosed with Alzheimer's. I knew it would get worse, and she needed help.

I had enough of this country by this time. I had a buyer, but they backed out. I tried to tell the bank what was happening, and they didn't want to hear it. I was dismissed as an annoyance, even though it is a law here that there should be at least one English-speaking person in each banking institution. More lies.

Finally, I have a couple who have been interested since last June. I contacted the bank to let them know, and they said they would hold proceedings.

Another lie. They did not, and apparently once in a system in Panama it's like trying to shake off a massive spider web.

It's not about money when you're in the system. It's about power and position. Nobody wants to take the money. They want the opportunity to use their stamp.

In the meantime, Alzheimer's waits for no one.

It took twelve days for the bank to give me a current balance due (I was of course charged extra because I am not from here. I call that, "walking while white"). It looked like something a twelve-year-old child had written up.

I try to do the right thing here, but this is a country where the right thing isn't always the way to move forward.

I am trying to get traction in a place without stability. It has taken everything in me to stick it out. Now, we find ourselves during another holiday time. Everyone wants to take a vacation and be with their families.

Alzheimer's is still progressing because it doesn't care.

This is supposed to be a time for gratitude, but I have a hard time finding things to be grateful for. Panama has stolen time from me and from my mother. They have stolen my right to be there for her. And they don't care.

How can I sit in gratitude when I am buried by selfish behavior in a culture that looks at the color of my skin and glares at me in the grocery line or on the street? I have been to many places where my skin is the lightest on the bus or in the stores, but never have I experienced a level of hate like in Panama.

There has been, in five years, only one business person who says what she means and means what she says. I will not name her, but I will say that if it wasn't for her stepping in as liaison, well, I just don't know if I could have handled anymore. I am grateful for her.

So I suppose I am grateful to be here to experience yet another stamp (not). I will continue to breathe in and out until I can't. Hopefully, I will get out of here and this situation will fade as just another bad dream. If I am lucky, I will be there in time for my mom.

I have always thought of the world as a place to experience as much as you can. Give what you can, help who you can, and move on.

Not in Panama. Not here. Not ever.

I lost my way in Panama. I lost hope, and I almost lost my life.

Like everyone, I look back on where I came from to help me better understand why I am, where I am. I thought I had shaken off patterns of turmoil and drama, but apparently I needed to go a bit deeper.

If I have learned anything in my life, it's that our experiences settle on us in layers. They come on in layers, and then heal in layers. As we heal or release upsetting or traumatic memories, it's like a layer peels off and we go to the next thing, and so on.

What I didn't understand at the time is that the upsetting memories had only been acknowledged, not released. It's like I looked back and held them and pet them like they still belonged to me. Then, I tucked them right back into that part of my brain where all of the unresolved issues stay, the amygdala. It's a tiny little part of the brain, but it holds so much.

I suppose writing things out helped me stay alive. I fought that twisted sick feeling of wanting to rescue my mom. That had been my job from so far back as a little girl and woven deep into the dysfunction that was my family.

In the middle of trying to find my way out of Panama, I lost my kitty girl Sailor to fibrosarcoma. I was guided to help her transition.

It felt like Panama stole her from me. It didn't really, but that's what it felt like. It was just another thing that happened before I could get out of that shit-hole of a country.

Panama was truly as "wild west" as it gets, with home invasions, kidnappings of expats, and haphazard shootouts in the middle of the street. There was trash burning on the side of the road, with flames so high they crossed over your car as you drove by, and protesters that threw rocks and burning tires to get their own way. Existence there was fiercely raw, full of unhidden corruption and death.

It is their normal, not mine.

When it was finally time to leave for good, I asked my friend Jennifer to help me make that transition from the house to the airport. I had boxes, and luggage, and I still had Jack, who did not travel well at all. I squished him into a small carrier, which was ridiculous for a Maine Coon cat.

At the airport, I was asked to pull him out a few times so his carrier could be searched. All the while, Panamanians in the line tried to press past me of course paying no attention to what was happening around them.

Jennifer was in charge of making sure I didn't freak out, and that I got on the plane in one piece. As soon as the wheels were up, tears rolled down my face. Jack mewed quietly for the first time in his life, and I began to believe I was going to make it.

Mom - 2018

A few of the many faces of Alzheimer's

Mom - 2015

Chapter 13

Arriving at my mom and step dads rebuilt farmhouse was a relief and a burden at the same time.

My mom didn't know who I was. That scared her, because most of the time she believed a stranger lived upstairs. I tried to keep her busy with walks and stories. I learned from the Alzheimer's Association to go where she was, mentally, so I tried to do that. She was frustrated and obsessed with her husband, and had to know where he was at all times.

She was also dealing with a serious case of Sundowners Syndrome, which is a state of confusion that manifests in the late afternoon and goes into the night.

Side Step….Rainbows and Roses

I knew the next part of my journey wasn't going to be all rainbows and roses, and I was right.

After my return to the United States, I gave myself nine days to prepare for the trip north to my mother's house. There were lists of items I would need just to get through daily life. Top priority was buying a car, computer, phone, and clothes that would keep me warm in blizzard-like conditions.

The state of my own health was less than good, but I was on a mission. I felt a need to get to my mom and assess her health, state of mind and living conditions. In my way of thinking it is the responsible thing to do, and besides I was her only option at the moment. Her sons were MIA once again.

It was now the end of February, 2015, and the northeastern part of the United States found itself in blizzard after blizzard, with no time to recover between storms. I packed the car and my unwilling cat Jack and I headed north from Pompano Beach, Florida.

Normally a fifteen hundred mile trip like this would take me two days. This trip would be far from normal.

This time it took seven days.

Jack has been my reason for breathing, and now I have put him in a situation most cats loathe. He let me know it, too. Every mile of this trip he screamed, shook and panted. My being an empath, I felt every ounce of his fear and heartbreak.

Together, we forged on, and the farther north we got, the more we found ourselves at the mercy of Mother Nature. I could not endure more than four hours of driving a day. With Jack screaming, and now the snow and ice blowing across the road, I had to choose my drive time wisely. We got as far north as Gettysburg, Pennsylvania, when a blizzard stopped us in our tracks.

What I noticed along the way is that the so-called pet friendly hotels were not as friendly to cats as they were to dogs. Infuriating as it was, I begged, pleaded and paid extra for my boy Jack to be in a safe place.

After the weather finally settled, we pressed on and made our way to the bare, colorless countryside that is the village of Morris, New York in the winter.

The devastating lack of color equaled the emotional hue of the disease known as Alzheimer's. It's a wake-less state of being taking over the elders of our country.

The first word that came to mind as I pulled into the driveway and met the new image of my mother was "bittersweet." Her body is shriveled and her spirit is crouched into a hidden part of her being that I later found, only comes out to fight.

I'm sure my appearance was just as ghastly, having gained weight and gray hair as I approach the half century mark this year. I'm certain I don't look like who I was when she last saw me.

Tragically, it doesn't matter, because, other than the fact that I am a guest in her house, she doesn't know who I am.

I didn't discover this until later in my stay. All I knew when I arrived was that I could not feel her energy when we embraced soul to soul At that moment, it was a mere wisp of a vibration.

I check my surroundings as best I can. My step-dad guides me to what would be my space upstairs. Before my arrival, I had been invited to use the entire upstairs floor, three bedrooms and a bathroom. They failed to mention they removed the upstairs kitchen I thought would also be mine to use.

It's OK, I think, because I will be downstairs most of the time, caring for my mom. No problem.

He put me in the smallest room upstairs, with bare walls and nothing but sheer curtains facing the highway. So much for undressing in private. The only television in the house is in their bedroom. There are no radios or stereos for music, except the one in his office.

I didn't know what to expect of course, but in the back of my mind I kept thinking, I would never treat a guest this way... especially one that has come to help in a time of need.

After unloading the car and getting Jack settled, I was expected to help get dinner ready at 4:30 PM. Dinner? At 4:30? What the hell?

That's when I learn the house is on his schedule, not hers. It was not the only narcissist red flag I saw along the way, but again, I think, it's ok; we will work it out. Mom has a reputation for keeping decent basics in the fridge, so I know I can do this.

I open the refrigerator door and mom starts pacing around me. She is uncomfortable that someone she doesn't know is in her kitchen. This is her domain, and I can see she is already getting frazzled at my presence, and I just got there.

As I look in the refrigerator I see moldy parts and pieces of things and multiple jars of the same items. There must be at least seven or eight salad dressings; five jars of the same kind of pickles. There are three jars of Miracle Whip, which I know my mother hates.

I can see now that I will have to watch him as much as I watch my mother, if for different reasons.

I open a deep kitchen drawer where they tell me the silverware will be and it looks as if a yard sale bomb went off. There are knives and kitchen gadgets that are mostly broken and / or will never be used. It's beyond a hoarder's clutter. All the upper cabinets lack doors and are cluttered with piles of dusty old wine glasses and mismatched tea sets. It's a hot mess, a non-functional hell-hole, but it's my mother's domain and she doesn't want it disturbed. Ugh.

As soon as the early bird dinner was over, her husband retreated to their bedroom. That was it for him for the evening. That meant this was normal, and that in the past she has been left to clean up and figure out the rest of the evening on her own.

This is a woman who can't put her own thoughts together. She is lost in her own home and has a husband so deeply drowning in his own denial, I found myself at a loss for words.

How do I approach all of these issues? I didn't know how to handle things, but I had to try my best.

It was the beginning of the end. I could no longer identify myself as Geneva LaVerne's daughter. I was now a live witness to what this disease has done to my mother.

As I grasp onto the idea of saving her, I feel her slowly slipping away from me and there is nothing I can do. It's a bad dream being played out in real time.

It will end up being a much shorter stay than I want, but ultimately it is not a choice that can be made by me. My heart slowly breaks as I realize the truth of these words.

As each day faded her stress level increased. Someone with Alzheimer's experiencing Sundowner's Syndrome has a need to move or adjust things constantly. She paced the house, took things out of cupboards and put them in drawers, or the oven.

People with Sundowner's often cannot sit still. It's also difficult for them to see, and therefore depth perception becomes an issue. I had read about these things, and now I was experiencing them first hand.

Oftentimes, I sat on the top of the stairs, waiting for the sound of the back door opening. It was terrifying to me to think she could end up in the creek on the side of the property, and nobody would know until it was too late.

I went to group meetings for Alzheimer's families and learned a lot from them. My mother's husband refused to go. I was there to help so that he could learn skills he would need, but he was not the least bit interested.

It was sad.

When I arrived, he took a much needed break; a road trip off on his own. I understood why he wanted to go. My mom was more than a handful, and he had a temper with a short fuse. I watched her while he went on what we called a "business trip." I set up some Skype time with her sisters so she wouldn't feel like she was alone in the house with a stranger.

It was never what I had wished for, but when the disease takes over, that's it. There is nothing that can be done. Her disease had progressed beyond the help of any drug.

She quickly became violent with me or anyone else that came to help. I tried my best to stay low-key and be a friend, but her focus could only be on where her husband was. It was very much the same as when I was younger: always about keeping track of the man in her life.

I was told it would be good to keep a journal while helping my mom, to keep track of her issues as she declined. Doctors ask a lot of questions, so the journal would help me have clear answers at the ready. It would also help me gain a better understanding of what she was experiencing, and learn from it.

Here are a few excerpts.

Journal….March 20th, 2015

At 4:37 AM I woke from a loud bang downstairs. I heard Tom and my mom in a muffled discussion. When I spoke to him this morning I asked if he heard a loud noise. He said yeah, that was him. He was angry at mom for leaving the water running after she went to the bathroom. He explained that there is no need for waste.

I reminded him that it's the disease that causes her to forget, and it's not her fault. He reminded me there is no excuse for waste, and said he was angry first at her, and then at himself for not getting up to check that the water was off.

As a side note, there are very strict rules about waste in this house. When you walk from one room to another you must turn out the light until you are ready to come back in.

Mom was never this way, so she would never remember. With Alzheimer's, she can't remember even if she wanted to. This makes it difficult, because it's better to keep it well-lit to help reduce mom's Sundowner symptoms.

Mom was really cold again all day. She talked about how awful a few people from her past were (they are deceased now). We looked through pictures, and she spoke of living on Grether Farm as a child. As she looked at the pictures of the house she was born in Zoe Oklahoma, she couldn't remember how they fit the kids in the house. It was so small.

We sang some silly songs. When I started cooking dinner, her mood shifted. This is where she taught me a phrase I had never heard of. She glared at me and said, "Go ahead, shit in the box; somebody will come along and cover it up."

It came from meanness, but it made me laugh. So she laughed too.

Journal....April 2nd 2015

The morning started out rough. Tom got up early as he always does. Today mom got up about twenty minutes after he did and immediately started looking for him. She began complaining about him being gone. I told her, "He is out feeding the chickens and he will be back." She complained a few more minutes and then went back to bed.

Later in the morning, before she came out, Tom explained to me that her oldest son (the criminal) may show up. She cried and said she wanted me out, and her house back. Tom took her for a walk after she ate breakfast.

I went to the Alzheimer's caregivers support group meeting. When I came back, things were semi-normal. I started making dinner, and asked mom if she wanted to help. I got a smart-ass negative response. I asked another question, and it was the same thing. Finally, I got her to peel and cut the parsnips and onions. Even though she saw a salad already made, she said, "Now what do we have to make a salad?" She did this with the fridge wide open about four or five times.

None of this is harmful, I just want to document her lack of ability to assess the situation.

After dinner, we looked through some papers and pictures Tom found. One document was a certificate of completion for an online cooking course mom earned. Other papers proved that my mom is of Cherokee bloodline. There were death certificates of great-grandparents, all of whom I knew nothing about. She snatched them from my hands after I started reading them out loud. I asked Tom to watch where she puts them, and in the meantime I will confirm with her sister Janetta if they are the documents she had been looking for. I called and they were not.

Geez, I had some serious flashbacks while going through this with her. She got angry if I cleaned, so I had to do it in the few hours her husband took her to the VFW for dinner. If I got caught cleaning, she would throw things at me -- more than dirty looks, mind you. She actually threw a knife at me one day.

That same day, I packed up all the sharp knives and hid them in my room. I had just survived six years in Panama; I could handle this.

Then I remembered from what I'd learned about Alzheimers that it wasn't about what I could or could not handle, it was about what she could handle. It wasn't about me and her, it was about her, and her new reality.

She was very uncomfortable that I was there. Eventually, she kicked me off the property.

Her asshole husband and I had a blowout argument about his anger outbursts (he would slam his fist down on the dinner table in frustration at her or slam doors and yell at her). I packed my car up to move to town. She gave me the boot the next day.

I called Adult Protection Services to ask what I should do, because she still needed to be cared for. They said I had to go.

My heart sunk as my mother stood on her back porch wielding a chair at me and screaming for me to get off of her land.

In true dramatic fashion, I screamed back, "I'm your only daughter." With nothing but rage facing me, I threw my house key (she used to lock me out, so I always had it around my neck) back at both of them and drove away south.

There was still snow and ice on the roads. Where would I go and what would I do?

I found a hotel about an hour south and started making phone calls to relatives and to agencies to see what rights I had as her daughter.

None. I had no right to take care of my mother, and in her madness she quite clearly didn't want me to take care of her.

This was the universe saying, "Look, you idiot, this is not your job. You have to let her go. This is the parting of the ways, so to speak."

I got fired by my own mom.

Again.

I can look back and chuckle at the drama of it all now, but it hurt like a son of a bitch then. When I got to that first hotel, I cried my eyes out. I ate crap food and then slept really hard. I had to heal from what I had gone through in not just the past however many weeks, but in the past forty-something years. It was time to shed the layers of pain and hurt.

I mean, seriously, I'm not a wimp. I am one of the toughest chicks I know. I could feel the weight of all of this emotion, and not just mine, but her's, too. The horrible family connection I had just opened back up was another issue, a festering pustule trying to permeate my life.

I didn't want any part of it. So as I drove south licking my wounds and listening to Jack, my cat, scream, I tried to tune in to spirit. I needed guidance, and fast. I had to find a place to land where I could heal and grow, and where I felt welcome.

I tried Saint Augustine for about a week. I rented a condo on the beach and yet never set foot in the sand. I couldn't find a place to live that wasn't astronomical in price and in a bad location.

I wandered around town and tried to get a feel for the place. There was something here, but I couldn't put my finger on it.

Unsuccessful in my search, I drove back south to where my friends lived in south Florida and tried to find a place to live there.

I didn't fit there, either. I wasn't connecting with the people I knew from before. I wasn't connecting with anyone.

It's how it is, though, isn't it? We all change. It's a constant. God was saying, "Don't try to fit in where you don't fit."

I had become disconnected… I felt like a wounded soldier just arriving home from Vietnam in the '60s. People looked at me, but didn't see me. I was there, but I was still under all of the layers of shit I had just been through.

I couldn't connect.

I spent a few long days driving back to St Augustine, where the universe finally said, "Feel this" so I did.

A condo kept popping up in a neighborhood that, online, looked old and beat up. It was different in person. I met with one of the owners, and as we stood on the front steps, overlooking the Intracoastal Waterway, I felt a vibration so intense it was distracting. I could barely have a conversation with her.

Finally, I looked at her. "Do you feel that weird vibration?"

She didn't. Oops.

This was a message for me. This was where I could plug in and recharge. Even though it was small and had old carpet, I knew it was where I needed to be.

There was one other problem that kept popping up. Every landlord wanted to run a credit check, but I was a literal ghost in the system. No credit cards. No credit, no credit history. I had cut up all my cards back in 1989.

She had no problem with that. A handshake and a signature on the lease, and we were OK. Jack and I had a new home.

I finally made my way to the beach and immersed myself in yoga for a short time. I focused on breath-work and channeling. I made a plan to grow my massage business by staying mobile. Mobile massage has kept me working in a way that I could spend extra time on clients if I needed to.

A space opened up at the local farmers' market. Space number eight, which represents abundance. The market gave me the opportunity to introduce myself to the community. I had my 10x10 event tent, my massage table, and some signage. It was almost like I knew what I was doing.

In the beginning I made the mistake of wasting money on advertising. This isn't "that" type of community. This town is old school, and very small in most ways.

I was lucky enough to be well-received at the farmers' market. I met and made some great connections and friends that I hope will be with me for many lifetimes to come. I have rescued and been rescued at this market.

I started my first season in Saint Augustine in the summer of 2015. It was hot. I mean Florida, sweat-your-balls-off hot. I didn't expect that kind of heat so far north.

I had a few get away trips and started learning about essential oils. The healing properties of therapeutic grade essential oils was blowing my mind. Well, let me rephrase that. They are healing unless you work for the FDA. In that case these oils don't do a thing for you. But boy don't they smell good?

Things seemed to be going along OK. I was building a clientele with my massage business. I made it through another hurricane season unscathed.

I still had my one good eye on my mom up north. Being where I was, I knew I could get to her if I had to. Her husband continued to leave her alone all day. I asked their neighbors for well checks every now and then. The wall had been put up, so I was trying hard not to bust it down and disturb the peace. If peace is what you call it.

In December, 2015, during a visit to the dentist, weird health shit started happening to me.

I needed a new crown. Reluctantly, I went in to have the work done. They built my crown on a computer in front of me. It seemed like a bionic tooth. Which was cool, except for the free blast of staph infection I picked up from their office.

About ten days later, my face blew up like a blowfish. I was in serious trouble.

It was Christmas. I had to work, but I couldn't show up for clients with my face looking like that. I reached out to every dermatologist in my area, but they were all booked or not taking new patients. I laid on my couch, continuing to swell up, and cry. How could this be the thing that takes me out? Shit.

I started dialing numbers for dermatologists in Jacksonville, and finally, I finally got in and got treated. It took weeks to heal, but that was just the beginning of a horrific year of skin conditions and bad health.

Rashes broke out on my arms. I thought it was eczema, which I was familiar with, but all of the ways I knew to heal eczema were not working.

Back to the doc I went, over and over again. More antibiotics! I tried oils and creams and tinctures. Nothing seemed to work except for prednisone, and that is something you don't want to put in your body if you can help it. I was repeatedly misdiagnosed, and prescribed drugs based on those errors.

"It's eczema!"

"No, wait, it's 'super eczema.'"

"No, it's dermatitis!"

"No, it's 'super dermatitis."

This demonstrates one of the reasons I have such an issue with western medicine. They are in the practice of pill pushing, not resolving issues.

To add insult to injury during the madness of mystery skin rashes, I was ignoring the healing process when it came to my relationship with my mom. Simply washing my hands of her wasn't working. My soul was broken and had not healed. I hadn't mourned the loss of the relationship I never got to have.

What happens when we don't grieve? We create a physical manifestation of the emotional body.

That's exactly what happened. I contracted pneumonia and the flu at the same time. From what I have learned in studying Chinese medicine there is a connection with the lungs when there is long standing unprocessed grief. My body manifested physical dis-ease from the emotional problem I had left unhealed.

The skin rashes wouldn't stop. I was beside myself.

Finally, I listened to a neighbor of mine at the farmers' market who did live blood analysis.

She discovered I had a systemic overgrowth of yeast in my body. Medically speaking, this is Candida, otherwise known as Candidiasis.

I didn't know anything about it, but I had to learn fast in order to get a grip on the disease, and on inflammation.

This meant going off of sugar, alcohol, and caffeine. A candida diet is strict, but as soon as I took sugar and carbs out of the equation, I healed.

Candida doesn't just go away, though. It takes time, and lots of probiotics, and switching supplements to kill the yeast as it adapts.

Candida is very "smart." It can actually hide in your blood cells. If you look at the live blood cells and don't see anything, but then disturb the cells, the little bastards pop right out of their hiding places.

No drinking and no eating out meant I had no social life. We don't realize that most things are prepared with sugar. I lost a lot of weight, which was great. Boring, but great.

A week in the hospital, and no one could diagnose this issue. It took a lady who had taken the time to learn how to do live blood analysis.

This goes back to what I learned years ago: the body never lies. So what was the emotional connection to candida?

According to my go-to resource, that little blue book by Louise L. Hay called "You Can Heal Your Body,"

"Feeling scattered, lots of frustration, and anger. Being demanding and untrusting in relationships. Great Takers."

It all made sense to me. Acknowledgement is a very important part of the process.

I credit a job I took on in my neighborhood with helping me segue into this phase of my healing work.

I was looking for a teaching venue when I stumbled by accident upon Riverside Cottages, a neighborhood assisted living and memory care facility.

I had hoped to find a conference room I could rent close to home. I pulled into the parking lot of what I thought was an office complex, because they didn't have a sign posted. I thought it was weird that their front door was locked, but they had a doorbell. Nothing happened when I rang it, so I thought, "Well, this is ridiculous," and started to walk away.

A lady ran out, shouting, "Wait, wait! We are open! Can I give you a tour?"

I didn't really understand, but I didn't want to be rude. As we walked in, I noticed what a beautiful space it was. Calming colors and beautiful lighting gave me the impression I was in a healing space.

Then, I realized it was an "old folks' home." Ugh. That wasn't what I was looking for.

But as I listened to the owner, Michelle Carmines, talk, I got a whole other message. Stay. They need you.

I said to Michelle, "You know, this isn't what I was looking for, but I think I'm supposed to be here."

I told her what I could do, and we made an agreement for me to come once a week for a few hours.

I fell in love with the elders.

I realized in a weird way this was a void that I was trying to fill. I wasn't looking to replace my mom, but I needed help in healing what happened in our relationship. The elders at Riverside helped point me in a good direction. I started in February, 2016, and a month and a half later the lung issues forced me to pay attention to the grief.

I had a close call with the other side yet again. I spent a week in the hospital hooked up to oxygen and breathing gadgets. I had to get out of there. I did not have insurance and could not afford being alive, much less a hospital stay. My dear friend and Reiki Master Joy, and our friend Teresa, came to take care of me for a week after I was released. It was a hard recovery, but once I could finally at least hold a bottle of water in my hands and climb my stairs, it was time to get back to work.

Side Step...It's All About The Energy

Energy is the root of all there is to this life and the universe. When we look at our physical bodies, its energy at the very core of our physicality. We are electric beings. Our souls are light energy that expand out, integrating with other souls, giving us proof we are now and have always been "One."

I'm gonna go "there" a little bit today because I am reminded constantly to look at things as energy.

How we move through life is our choice. We choose to turn left or turn right and interact, or not, with those around us. We can choose to be open and accept the presence of a new experience in our daily living.

Being in the presence of new energy doesn't mean it has to change your belief system, but wouldn't it be cool if it altered our level of vibration. I believe it does. I also believe that thinking positively on this very subject ripples out and changes the way we affect those around us.

I recently opened myself to a neighbor from whom I originally received a closed-off vibe. It was as if there was no way "in" no matter how nice or helpful I was. That door was closed to newbies.

Instead of hanging on to the idea that, "its me" and "I don't belong," I accept where I am and where they are, energetically. I am learning to stay my course, and that's shifting the flow of my life. I feel as if I've become available to a smoother way of being.

Once I did that, the neighbor approached me about clearing out the negative energy from a property she owns.

There is our connection: energy. It always comes back to that.

I found the same thing to be true of a group of therapists, body-workers if you will, who are connected by their use of the same healing modality. Several years back I was very connected and in their loop. However, I took a left turn and ended up out of the country and, therefore, out of the loop.

I am back now, after wrestling many demons and rising like a phoenix from the ashes. It was an epic battle for which I can never express the intensity to someone who hasn't been in the trenches. It is truly a miracle I am here, and I sit in gratitude every day.

Upon my return I went to reconnect with that group, only to be made to feel like I didn't belong. Or I should say, I allowed myself to feel like I didn't belong. This was a huge wake-up-call, and I found myself wanting to lay down and feel sorry for myself. After all, I was still incredibly raw from the battle I was just in. I didn't have the strength for yet another challenge.

Instead, I took a moment (in reality, a few weeks) to go back to the thought of being in the energy.

I know where I am and what I am about. I know that Source or the Higher Power (I call this God) is guiding me to simply "Be" and not hang on to old ego-driven ways. Embracing the energy of who I am and what I am here for makes me realize I am part of the whole. Whether or not I connect with the group of therapists doesn't matter. I bring light energy and love to the table. I am the light, and so are they.

My neighbor is also the light. Accepting who I am as light energy helps me see the light connection -- the energetic connection -- to others around me. It feels right. It keeps life moving at a higher vibration, and that is where I am most comfortable; where I call "home" in my heart.

As I set about doing my morning rituals today, I kept smelling and tasting cigarette smoke. I don't smoke, but one of my spirit guides was a heavy smoker and drinker when he was in the physical. This was his way of helping me sense who was trying to give me guidance.

I sat down to connect with this guide. He helped confirm everything I have been feeling and experiencing in the past six months. He reminded me of Annie, a woman who created an invocation to the light. For quite a while now I thought I was remembering her invocation, but I inadvertently created something different yet similar: "I am the light; you are the light; we hold the light together."

I say thank you to both Annie and the spirit that gave me confirmation of those thoughts about energy and how we are constantly evolving. From the core of my being, I am grateful to be a part of this moment, this learning experience.

With only the occasional bouts of candida and staph relapses, things are better in the health department, but geez, 2016 and 2017 were rough years.

Chapter 14

It was 2017 and the tail end of my health struggle when I added a few new healing modalities to my tool belt.

I stumbled across Dr. Benjamin Perkus' Aroma Freedom Technique, wherein you breathe in Young Living essential oils while focusing on and processing an upsetting or traumatic memory. I learned about it via video a Facebook video

At first I thought, "Ugh. Not another PHD saying how we can 'heal our bodies by letting go.' Fuck. This isn't as easy as it sounds, and I have done a ton of therapy to even be where I am now."

I didn't want to listen to yet another New Ager spouting stuff we already know, but spirit had other plans. I kept hearing, "Just sit down and watch the video."

So I did. I took notes the entire time. He talked about how our unresolved and unregulated memories are left unprocessed and stored in the part of your brain called the amygdala. When we breathe in the essential oil, it passes through the olfactory and enters the limbic system, the "seat of emotions," and actually relaxes the amygdala so the unresolved memory can then be processed.

I tested this technique on a particularly annoying childhood memory.

When I was young, my uncles and stepfathers used to call me "fatso." They thought it was funny. It was not funny, and I was not fat. I was a little girl, and they were idiots.

They made me feel so awful, as an adult I could never hear or say the word "fatso" without feeling nauseous and like I immediately needed to throw up.

So I thought, "I'm gonna try this guy's theory."

I had all of the oils, and I had the time. I easily went through the process and did have an emotional release. I can now say that word without the physical reaction.

This is great for intention setting, because it helps remove the negative voice that tells you things are not possible, and that you aren't good enough. It helps you process that unresolved stuff that blocks you from getting what you want. It is a great technique, and anyone can buy the book and walk through the process as long as you use the correct essential oils.

This technique had such a profound effect on me, I immediately ordered the book and read it in a day. I then took Dr. Perkus' certification course, and became the first certified Aroma Freedom Technique Instructor in the state of Florida. I taught classes and certified students of my own and of Dr Perkus'.

I still occasionally teach, and still use this technique on myself and with my clients as needed.

2017 became about healing, teaching, and expansion. It also brought Hurricane Matthew. Matthew was no Katrina, but most of downtown Saint Augustine flooded. The Northeast coast of Florida is not usually in the path of these storms, but apparently, we needed a purge.

After checking with my peeps (spirit), I chose to stay for this hurricane. It's not for everyone, so if you are told to evacuate, please listen. The only thing that makes it different for me is that I have nothing to lose. I have no children or close family; no spouse or significant other to worry about me. I'm OK with that. Instead of getting wound up by the fear the weather stations brought on (geez, they really piss me off), I chose to stay and hold space with my kitty Jack.

Piece of cake; piece of pie.

After all of the crazy weather settled and fall set in, I went north to Knoxville, Tennessee to teach a class and speak at a conference. Before I left, I received a message from spirit while working on a client of mine. She is also psychic, and at the end of her massage she said I showed her that I was helping people cross over. She said it's not for everybody, but clearly it was easy for me. She wasn't speaking about people who are alive. She was talking about people who were in-between places. Limbo, for lack of a better term.

I said, "Yes, that's true," without even blinking an eye. But did I really know this?

Yes, on a soul level, I did. It takes time for our physicality to catch up with the speed at which we work on a soul level. So I parked the information she gave me, knowing it was true.

I got this message three times. The third and final time it made me pay attention, I was outside of Knoxville at a "healing circle" with another healer I was traveling with. This group of people got together to assist those needing help in their transition.

There was no explanation of what was going down. I sat, open to the process, and felt and heard spirit without question. This shamanistic work is very comfortable for me. We call in the light and create the space for the souls to complete their journey. These are souls that had traumatic or unexpected endings and got lost or confused in the transition.

This was not in my physical vocabulary until the moment I sat in this circle. It was my third message, and my big nudge that it was time to start doing the work.

I didn't know what to call it until I did some reading and learned that, in Greek mythology, one who guides souls to the afterlife is called a psychopomp. I can't stand the name -- it sounds ridiculous to me -- so I just call it "release work."

I have continued this work in northeast Florida, and even into southern Georgia. As an empath, there are times I feel a density in an area, and I feel that all over Saint Augustine, Florida. Along with that feeling, I often get visions of what transpired. Then, a lead spirit will step forward and help gather the others when it's time to move on and complete their journey.

I know it sounds batshit crazy, but it's real, and it's an honor to be part of the process. One of the books that helped me better understand this process is "Death

Walkers," by David Kowalewski, PhD. Another is "Cave and Cosmos" by Michael Harner, but trust me, there is not a lot of information out there about this.

When doing release work, I first ask what area is in need, and I call in and channel spirit before doing the clearing. I write down any message the soul wants to bring forward before they complete the transition. Once I call in the light and relate the message, I finish with a prayer. As they leave, sometimes I can feel whispers of kisses on my cheeks, or pinches at my feet and ankles.

It's a beautiful feeling, and such an honor to be a part of their transition. This work does so many things beyond helping them move forward. It also clears the energy where they were "stuck."

Most days, I shake my head and think, "How in the hell did a person like me get to be where I am?" Look at what I have lived through. I am still growing and figuring out how to be here and help other people.

The one person that I wanted to help the most, I couldn't. I was set up for a long goodbye.

Side Step....Strange Love

There is no stranger love than the love between a mother and daughter. It's a love that is so powerful on so many levels, it's almost unimportant to have the physical body there to carry it. It is strong enough to hold its own. Even when the lower emotions enter into the picture, like blame, guilt or hate, it doesn't matter, because there is this crazy connection that starts from the womb. Trust me, I have run the gamut with my mom. Anger and hurt were the strongest emotions I had for her for years.

Then, I started to understand myself, and who I am with or without her. I started to understand, as I came to be the age she was when I held the negative emotions, and I get it now. The all-knowing light bulb moment comes on every now and then, and I have a better understanding of why she wanted to escape her life.

I didn't realize I was affected on such a deep level when she locked herself in her room. I felt not only her pain, but also my hurt and confusion.

What a mess.

Now that she is older, and I am older, and we have both gone through so much healing in our lives and in ourselves, I hope she feels the love she didn't get to feel when she was younger. I try to send it to her from a distance as often as I can, everyday. As I walk through the house and she comes to mind, I feel her pull and I say to her, out loud, "I love you, mom." I know on some level she hears it. This past week, I received confirmation.

I am still handling the last bits of business here in Panama before I can return. So even though I know that mom can't hold a steady conversation, I hope she receives the loving energy I am sending her from the core of my being. I want her to know that no matter what we went through in our relationship, the good, the bad and the ugly, she deserves to feel unconditional love.

My mother is currently in a state of Alzheimer's. She is what I call "floating along in the in-between world." Before I hang up on the phone with my mom, I always say, "I love you and I will check in with you in a few days." This past week, she said, with clarity, "You check in with me all of the time."

A massive feeling of overwhelming joy passed through my body. I asked her, "Mom do you feel it when I send you love? Are you feeling it?"

She said yes, she feels it.

That was one of the most beautiful moments of confirmation I have ever had. It will carry me through to her end, when she is ready to make her transition. Whether it's ten days from now or ten years, that will do me just fine.

I attribute that feeling of love to that mother-daughter connection. Although we didn't have a smooth ride, I am grateful I was conceived out of love. Not the love of her husband ,but the love of her soul mate. I am so grateful to have been a part of that.

In all of the time I had been moving forward in the healing arts and mediumship work, I never forgot or turned off the connection to my mom.

I couldn't call her because she didn't know how to answer the phone. She couldn't call me because she didn't know how to dial. She couldn't have a conversation because she didn't know who I was.

This killed me.

Her husband was no help. In her mental state, he regularly left her alone, and this became dangerous.

In 2018, I finally got word he had placed her in a home. What did she need? What medication was she on? How was she settling in? He provided very limited information. All of these things didn't matter to him, but they mattered to me.

Apparently mom kept trying to escape and "get home." She became more difficult, and was removed from the facility. I never found out if it was his choice, or if the facility requested it.

He placed her in a shit-hole institution in the sticks of upstate New York. They had very bad ratings and staff had been arrested for abuse the year before.

The worst thing about my mom's idiot husband is that he is cheaper than cheap except when it came to his own mom, who was placed in a beautiful, well-kept place run by Masons. He could have placed my mom there, but he chose not to.

On the upside, it shortened my mom's life. I know that sounds like a horrible thing to say, but living in the in-between place that is Alzheimer's is not easy, and I would rather see her go in peace than be in that,"state" for an extended period of time.

It killed me, knowing I had no power when it came to her well being. I had to try though, didn't I? I am such a twisted warrior. I made a plan, and followed through.

I flew to Albany, New York and drove to my mom's facility in Cooperstown. Nobody knew I was coming. If you ever have concerns about where a parent is placed, I highly recommend this. If nobody knows you are coming they can't prepare a fake living situation.

I heard the screams of residents as I walked into the facility. I didn't get too excited about this because I've heard this before. It's not unusual. It doesn't necessarily mean they are being hurt, it's a state of mind; how residents sometimes express frustration. If there are enough caregivers, residents can be attended to, and calmed down. This was not the case in this facility. There were lots of residents, and not enough help.

When I walked into the common room and found my mom, I was shocked at how quickly she had changed. Her body was a shell. She could no longer see well, and she was, like most elders, cold all of the time.

There was no fat on her body because she didn't eat anything but pureed food. Her false teeth had been lost in the move between facilities. It is common for elders with

Alzheimer's to pull out their dentures and put them somewhere. I had no idea where moms went to but maybe they are with all of the clothes that I bought her. In the heart of winter she was wearing capri pants and no shoes. Checking her room, all of the clothing I bought and shipped to her was gone. She had nothing left that was identifiable.

She didn't care, because she didn't know the difference. It still pissed me off. I think this is one of the reasons I am so impressed with Riverside Cottages, because residents there maintain a sense of integrity. In my mom's room there was nothing there that said, "This is the room of Geneva McMillen," despite the fact that I had given her family pics to create some feeling of it being a kind of home for her.

I grabbed my mom and we walked into another, quieter common room. I brushed her hair and held her hands. I took pics to send to her sisters and her sons. I took a video as well, so there was something for the family to connect with. This had been the job of her husband.

He failed, beyond even my expectation.

My mom was a handful, and while I didn't envy the caregivers taking care of her, I did expect that they actually did the job of changing her adult diaper, but they put off changing her because she would fight and scream at the top of her lungs.

This is fear; pure fear. I could feel it miles away, but up close and personal, it tore my heart out. She was experiencing childhood fear that had never healed.

Think about someone that had been molested as a child and are now mentally and emotionally that age once again. It's horrific. If the facility had the staff to dial in her meds, it may have been a slightly better experience for her.

About a month or so after our final goodbye, my mom died in that horrible place in Cooperstown, New York on April 26th, 2018.

I am glad she went, but I wish she had been treated with more dignity in the end.

Every time I hold an elders hand to massage them I do my best to treat them with as much respect and love as I possibly can.

It's what I wanted for my mom but could never give.

Side Step....The Many Faces of Death

I see many different faces of death in the work that I do. Some are peaceful and smooth. Others are ragged and angry until they finally give in. The faces I see are not just physical, but the energy that emotes from the soul going to the next place. It will be different for all of us.

One of the most beautiful deaths I have experienced was of an elder client named Grace. Her last moments were spent with her daughters all around her. Yes, there was a separation of body and soul that can sometimes be hard to watch, but those who loved her brought so much joy to the room, she floated on a bed of angelic roses through the thin veil between this world and the next one.

My wish is that we all have that experience, but that is not how it works.

My own mother's death was nothing like Grace's passage. I wish it had been, but that was not the journey she chose. It had to be her way.

Lately I have been getting visits by the owl, the traditional messenger of death/transition, including last night. I knew a client of mine had finally let go to make her journey. I have to say, she was a tough little shit and ran her family ragged. She got me, too or I wouldn't be writing this piece at 3:44 in the morning.

It is in her honor, and also to those that have passed in the last little while, including my mother Geneva, that I write this.

The Many Faces of Death

Your eyes are clear

They see me

Your heart is deep

As deep as the sea

As you let go of this physical body

You expand

As the soul that you are

Do you feel it now?

The pull to pure joy, pure love

Its powerful enough to carry you

The rest of the way

The way you haven't wanted to go

But it's here now

Hold on to the hands that are reaching out for you

Hold on to the love that is seeping into your soul

There is no room for anger now

Its vibration no longer resonates with you

Love, pure love

Peace, pure peace

When you finally let go of the anger

The fear, the judgement and the rage

Source fills your soul

You float into the next realm of existence

The realm of Gods beauty after the human experience

Let go of the shell of what you can no longer be

Feel the pulse of your soul

It belongs to the flow

The oneness that is the universe

Outside of the physical being ness

Its beauty is you, and you are now

You are everything

Do you see me?

Do you see you, now that you are there?

Do you feel everything now?

Isn't it everything you never thought it could be?

It is

It is oneness

I am overjoyed for your time to be now

In that weightless light being existence

Honor the journey that you took

Here on this earth plain

It wasn't easy

It wasn't pretty

The anger you held for so long withered your little body.

It ate you up with the resentment that was the cancer in your life

Your face of death wasn't beautiful

but it was yours

And mine will be mine

Even with blood spewing from your swollen body

The journey you chose was yours and it held a beauty and fierceness of its own

The sacred owl came and told me you were going now

We will all feel your power from the other side

Light and love, peace and joy little one

Breathe in your sigh of relief

It's time for you to shine

Chapter 15

I often stand at my front door looking out over the river while giving thanks for so many things. One early morning in July, I stood, coffee mug in hand, and felt as if I was saying goodbye to the person I was.

I was now guided to welcome my new self into this life.

The sun was just breaking over the horizon as I thought, "This is it. I will never be in this moment and be the way I am right now. I won't ever think how I think right now at this moment. Something big is about to happen. Change is coming."

It felt so good. I embrace change as my one constant. It's that swirl of energy that moves in and out of your space and around your being that can never be tamed.

I love change because it's what I know best. In 2005, at the age of forty, I came to a crossroads and went back to school to get a degree and learn massage therapy. Who knew that it would lead me down a path of communicating with spirit? In my younger years I would have said, "You're off your rocker if you think I'm gonna sit around and talk to dead people."

But that is exactly what happened. Not at the snap of a finger, but slowly, my life changed in a way that led me to know it was possible. Then, God sent me an angel who told me to get my shit together. The angel said that it was time to stop messing around, and focus on giving back. This is why I came back from death at the age of twenty-nine.

So, early in the morning on July 3rd, I found myself saying goodbye to Picasso the massage therapist, Reiki Master and channel of soul charts. I was open to this new beginning and had no idea what to expect, but I knew to stand in faith no matter what. I trust God and spirit to get me where I need to be. I just have to stay out of my own way so these things can happen.

A few months earlier, the volume turned up on my ability to sense certain things. I was seeing, hearing and feeling everything more intensely than before. I knew I needed to learn what to do with this, and that I couldn't just play in the energy. It was time to help people with this new thing that was happening. Whatever it was.

Recently, I learned about a place in Stansted, England, called Arthur Findlay College. It's the oldest and most sacred place for the advancement of spiritualism and psychic sciences... sort of a "Hogwarts" for mediums. I could never have afforded it at the time, but when all of this happened, some very special people gifted money to me (sneakily I might add).

I didn't know what to do or say, and then all of the signs fell into place. It became so clear. I knew exactly what to do. I said goodbye to everything I had learned so far and hello to the British way of evidence-based mediumship.

Holy shit. I hadn't been thrown into the deep end of the pool, I jumped! Because I had faith, I realized I wouldn't drown.

It had been one of the hottest summers ever in England. There had been no rain for more than a month, and everything was wilting, including the tutors at Arthur Findlay College. However, the British way is to have a stiff upper lip and keep up the standard in which they were accustomed to teaching.

I signed up for a week-long class and was placed with a tutor by the name of Janet Nohavec. She is an ex-Catholic nun from New Jersey. After watching my classmates stand on a platform and demonstrate mediumship skills, I was afraid I had made a big mistake, but Janet guided me to connect with the part of myself that could do what everyone else was doing.

I was the least experienced of my class, but I kept saying to myself, "Well shit, I'm here to learn and to grow, so I better get out of my own way."

It wasn't easy. I had to listen to Simon James, the lead tutor, go on and on about how American mediums are reckless and irresponsible, and we don't know what we are doing. He would of course assert that the British need to come over to America and teach us a thing or two.

After about the third day, I was pissed off and was about to stand up and say something... then I looked back at how I was taught. Most of the channeling lacked evidence because we never asked spirit to be specific. Simon was right. There is so little evidence based mediumship, and an absolute over-abundance of psychic channels like myself. It doesn't mean we are wrong in what we are doing, just that we have no foundation on which to base the information that comes through.

Things changed for me in those few days. I listened, and stopped pushing away this traditional way of thinking. I opened myself up to a new way of communicating. It's not completely smooth for me yet, but I'm learning to sit in my own power and expand. I have learned to invite spirit into my space in a more respectful and traditional way.

This is the change I felt so deeply as I stood at my door looking out over the water that peaceful morning. I said goodbye to a way that I knew I was so comfortable with, and hello to a language that holds a higher frequency that gives me the ability to be of service to people and to spirit.

What a powerfully blessed feeling that is.

I have embraced the change that happened in England, but it's been hard to slow it down. I will never forget hearing my teacher say, "Now Picasso don't go back and try this platform work at home. You must sit in the power first."

I nodded and agreed. Sitting in the power and expanding my soul for what would come in the future would be the thing to do.

So what did I do? I sat in the power and sat in the power and then looked around and said, "Shit, is that enough?"

It wasn't.

I started with meditation and sitting in the power, followed by working with people one on one a few weeks after coming back from England. I wanted to practice, and I did. I did my regular checking in with my peeps.

I can see the eyes of Simon James roll back into the back of his head, while Janet Nohavec is shaking her head, "No NO NO! Have we taught you nothing?"

I felt the growth and expansion. I heard and saw more than ever before. So, I tried doing platform work with a group of local ladies one of my clients set up for me. I explained to them what my intention was, and what I wanted to accomplish. I said, "I'm going to get quiet and centered for a few minutes and invite spirit in. I will then try to connect spirit with whoever it is they want to speak with, and or give a message to."

There is nothing worse for a medium than pressure. It's a killer, and you can totally tank if it takes you over. The first spirit came through very clearly and concisely. The connection was made, the message was good, and I started to calm myself a bit. Whew!

But just when I wasn't looking, it all went to hell in a handbag. Spirit came through, but nobody could connect with the information.

After about six tries, I said, "OK, ladies, that's gonna do it for me."

I was embarrassed and ashamed, and truly bummed out. Was I not meant to do this work? Why had I taken that trip and learned what I learned? As this reel played in my head, I heard, very loudly, "You must walk before you run."

Janet Nohavec told me this. I thought I had walked long enough. I wanted to run with spirit. But even as I write these very lines, my lamp light flashes: confirmation.

I know I'm right.

So, more sitting in the power. Ugh. More meditation and quieting the mind.

Stillness is necessary. If you could ever see what's in my head, you would know it never shuts up. Now add all the extra new noises, and its a cluster-fuck.

I honored this message, though, and finally got quiet. I regrouped with the same ladies and sat with them in one-on-one scenarios.

It worked beautifully.

Thank God and the spirits, because I was getting ready to look for a nine-to-five job soon and just pack it in. I'm glad I didn't.

As frustrating as it is, I do find stillness calming and healing for my heart and soul. Every now and then, the human part of me comes back and says, "How can you do this and still pay the bills? How can you help people in this way when sometimes they won't even acknowledge the message for them is absolutely accurate?"

I am learning to trust. I didn't say I was good at trust, but it is the word my mentor Lisa Williams whispered to me during one of our class lessons. "Trust."

As you recall, trust wasn't even part of my family vocabulary. You couldn't trust anyone in the family to step up and do the right thing without some kind of drama happening. But we get through it, don't we? It's what makes us who we are.

I want women, and men of course, to trust their basic instincts. If it looks like shit and smells like shit, it's gonna be shit. Don't step in it or keep it by your side. Don't put its number in your purse to call it later, because it's going to do nothing but stink up your life. There are options for us. Listen to them.

Check in with your peeps, be they spirit, God, the angels, or someone that is living and has at least half a brain.

When I was young, I always dreamed that someone would come and take me away from all of the violence of my family. However, had that happened, I wouldn't be who I am. I had to learn where my line was going to be. I had learn about boundaries, and how to tell people about to do me harm to fuck off. I learned, in all the madness, that I mean something, or I wouldn't be here.

You mean something, too, or you wouldn't be reading this story, looking for answers, just like I did.

I had to die to get those answers, but that was my journey. I am still learning and developing as a woman and healer.

People have come and gone in my life. Some would say I don't give people as many chances as I should, but I am simply listening to what's OK for me. I have friends who sometimes say I hate men, or that because of my past experiences, I am too hard on men. That is just not the case. I simply will not be owned or treated less than just because a man steps into my world.

Remember to smell it first. If it smells like honesty and truth, then it's worth keeping around. I love people who are willing to see the whole picture; the big picture. No, I don't hate men. Of course I don't. I am not willing to give energy and coddle men or women that find the need to seem more important than me. If they are just another idiot trying to dominate your life, then send them packing.

I now have the courage to say goodbye if the friendship is not a good match. It's OK to let people go if you feel the relationship isn't reciprocal.

This does not mean I don't care, but I am on a mission to help myself and to serve spirit in the best way I can. If you look deeper this can be a teaching moment for you. Look at all the shit I lived through and it did not prevent me from learning how to love. My traumas did not prevent me from taking charge of what is right and good for me. Trauma is fucked up, but you can turn it into something teachable.

We all have the right to a God connection, a spirit connection. I have yelled at God on many occasions, demanding the madness end. It is usually at that moment he sends me something to help me understand why I am in a particular situation. God gave me strength to endure the trauma.

I am a warrior. I am strong and fiercely courageous. I am also soft and sincere and vulnerable, like anyone else. If I judge you, I am wrong in judging. It is the same when you look at me and say, "What is wrong with her?" Look closer, then look in the mirror, and you will see what you are meant to see at that moment.

So why did I need to write my story? When I started, I wanted to convey to women mostly like myself that they could make it out of a bad situation. I wanted them to know survival is possible.

Moreover, I want people to know they can change their belief system, or create their own belief system. It doesn't have to be derived from a holy book that some men wrote and changed over the years.

I want people to know it is important to dream big, and change your path. I want people to know that the answer is in the healing, in the forgiveness and understanding you gain as you grow in this human experience. Just because I was raised in a shithole doesn't mean I was meant to stay in that same shithole. You have options. You just have to fight, claw, and worm your way out of it.

Fight for your right to survive. You can break whatever cycle has been handed to you. Get creative, and remember you are worthy of so much more love and appreciation than what you are accepting now.

Believe in yourself. It's hard to learn to look in the mirror and say, "You are a beautiful and deserving soul."

I have done the mirror work at the written advice of Louise Hay. I'm sorry, Louise, but that didn't work for me.

I tried twenty-one days of affirmations. Everyday, looking in the stupid mirror and saying something I just didn't believe.

You can't just say that shit. You have to believe it for change to happen.

I had to let go of the voice inside that says, "You are not worthy." It wasn't really me saying it. In fact the "voice" was those memories and experiences from earlier abuse in my lifeI had not yet resolved.

It's about resolution, not revolution. Let everything go that isn't helping you or those around you.

I sometimes now look in the mirror and find myself distracted by how I have aged. I see my scars, wrinkles and spots, not to mention hair where there shouldn't be hair. Then I focus, and I look deeper and say, "OK girl, you made it this far. Now what are you going to do?"

I see the strength and power that bothers some and inspires others. I see my unraveled self. I am willing to share so there can be healing. Do I make mistakes? Yes and often, but it doesn't kill me. I am no longer guarding a house of cards on the verge of collapsing and destroying my ability to survive.

There is just me, at that moment, staring back and me.

What I was born into was not loving and stable and comfortable, but that was to be my journey until I was ready to change it. Nobody would do that for me, except me.

When I was younger, I cried for someone to come and rescue me from the constant state of chaos that was my childhood. That was never to be. I had to learn to fight back and win, myself.

As a warrior, I had to learn to heal the wounds received in my fights. I had to learn that there are other ways of doing things. Surviving rape and molestation taught me to heal, and to understand the "why" behind the experiences.

As Pierre Teilhard de Chardin wrote, "We are not human beings having a spiritual experience. We are spiritual beings having a human experience."

The human experience can be dirty, and gritty, and nasty. It can also be loving, and kind, and generous. We are here for all aspects of the human experience. Therefore we need many lifetimes to have those experiences. It's about the intensity of our thoughts, feelings and traumas along the way.

What would God have us do? Breeze through completely unscathed? How would we be able to understand the importance of forgiveness if we never had anything to forgive? How could we know the depth of hate and rage if we had no peace or love for comparison?

What would I say to the neighborhood boy who pinned me down and tried to rape me when I was eight? On one hand, I'm glad I was able to kick you in the nuts and I hope it caused you not to have children you would steer completely wrong in life. But I know that is not fair, because you came into this life to be that boy who would try to rape that girl. What I would say is that I hope you made it to adulthood and gained an understanding that you can be more than a taker of a little girl's virginity. I hope you realized the physical aspect of your masculine body is more than just getting a hard-on and spreading your seed. My hope is that you got to experience holding a hand out, and that you helped lift someone up who was down. Or better yet, I hope that you got to be down, and learned how to receive the hand that reached out to you. There is more to learn, sometimes, in the receiving than the giving.

What would I say to the pedophile who was my mother's father? I detest what you did to me and so many other little girls. However, I honor that you completed so much karmic debt in this lifetime. When our relationship was one of attacker and victim, we had a soul connection that was more than we could have known at the time. This is part of Walking the Way into forgiveness. I do forgive you, and I understand that you were here to experience trauma from the driver's seat, as the deviant.

What would I say to the man who raped me when I was fifteen? If it hasn't yet played out, you will have to feel the same thing down the karmic payback line. For that, I am sorry for you. You created more shame where shame had already existed. I have spent years of wondering why a man can feel the need to fuck women who don't want to be fucked. I say to you: there is more to the human experience than sticking your dick where it isn't invited. If it was pleasure you sought, there are other ways.

I am a powerful woman. Know that your abuse took only half of my life. It did not take my whole life. You failed. As a warrior, I can say I win, and you lose.

What would I say to the propeller that chopped up my face? Thank you. Although you destroyed the vanity I held as my Leo self, you forced me to walk out of my body. You took my life. This created pain and suffering from which I would have to learn to heal.

Isn't that the lesson here? Learn to heal. Learn to forgive, and be blessed in the rest of your journey. I died so that I could learn to live. The blessing is that I got to see and feel while I was on the other side.

While I am grateful now, I wasn't always. Staring at the scars on my face every time I look in the mirror has become just a part of my routine. I know I am not only the scars, but the story that goes along with them.

I often say this to the elders I work on as they complain about what their skin looks like at their age. Your blemishes, marks, and scars are the map of your life. They tell your story.

One of my all time favorite movies is Thelma and Louise. I understand how they got where they were, and how and why they went the way they did.

These are my favorite lines from that movie:

THELMA
You awake?

LOUISE
Guess you could call it that, my eyes are open.

THELMA
I'm awake too. I feel awake.

LOUISE

Good.

THELMA

I feel really awake. I don't recall ever feeling this awake. You know? Everything looks different now. You feel like that? You feel like you got something to live for now?

I can't even tell you how many times I have thought of driving off a cliff or into something bigger than me that would take me from this world into the next. There are some days it just feels like enough is enough.

It's usually right about then that God shines a little light into the darkness. Oftentimes, on those days, I feel awake. Really awake. After walking through all of the things I shared with you in these pages, I think I feel even more awake, if that's possible.

It can be difficult to understand where our intel is coming from when we're in that awakened state. For me, sometimes it's books or google, but mostly it's spirit. The lines of communication stepped a bit farther into the fifth dimensional state of being.

This is all the more reason to be mindful of your thoughts and words. We have heard over and over that words are very powerful. It is true. We have all experienced the phenomenon of getting a phone call or card or other communication from someone we had just been thinking of. The law of attraction and how to call things that we want to experience has entered into mainstream awareness. So you may understand when I tell you my lessons these days are not as much from books as they are from spirit.

I'm learning from my clients' departed loved ones. I stay as open as possible. I allow astute energy in so that I can give messages from spirit to clients willing to receive. Mostly, spirit helps me get the point across in kind and creative ways.. I'm relatively new at the process, so we are working together to create a system that works for us.

I keep looking for a mentor for this part of the process but it seems my real mentors are not in the physical. There is no note taking. There is just doing, and being in the moment.

The reality for me is, as an empath, if I'm in your presence, I feel everything you feel. When spirit is present I hear what they are telling me. Every now and then, not often, a spirit will voice themselves out loud.

I see things that are not visible to everyone. I no longer assume it's my imagination. Pets of loved ones are coming through quite often now… living pets, so I don't know what is happening here. Perhaps with pets getting ready to transition it's like when someone is in an altered state such as Alzheimer's, and they can kind of play on both sides.

For example, a parrot came through when I was working on a veterinarian. The parrot was in trouble because of her human's chaotic state. The parrot's feathers were falling out, and she needed help. All I could do in this situation is pass the message to the veterinarian to please have the parrot's owner come for a massage or reading.

All I can do is pass the message, even though sometimes I want to cram the message down their throat...

Probably the most frustrating thing is when a client asks for a reading, they are presented evidence it is their loved one, and yet they continue to question whether it's really them.

That just makes me want to cry in my martini, but I have learned from my mentor, medium Lisa Williams to say, "Fuck It."

I think that's why I like her so much. Lisa is a no-bullshit, phenomenal psychic medium. She teaches from experience. Having been in the industry for many years, she has stood up to the political crap and the liars, cheats, and thieves in the industry.

Spirit told me this a few months earlier, but I must have needed to hear it from Lisa to really get the lesson: It's not about me. It's about being the voice for spirit when at all possible.

Lisa helped me and five other students do something rare at LilyDale, the spiritual community in western New York. She gave us the opportunity to serve spirit as student mediums in the auditorium.

This is not something that happens often. You must be a registered medium to serve spirit at LilyDale. I said, "Fuck it. Sign me up."

Walking with other students to the auditorium, I heard the conversation in my head:

Picasso what are you thinking? Why are you doing this? You don't have anything to prove here.

Then I heard and felt my mom whisper in my ear, "Because that's just the kinda girl you are."

This is something I have said since my first sail across the Atlantic, many years earlier, when people asked why I did something so adventurous.

"That's just the kind of girl I am."

No fear. I was brought back to live this life and to be of service -- to give back, and to help the less courageous find their courage.

It's important to address the ongoing abuses taking place in homes and to help women take their power back. This is not a man's world. Remember what we already know: as women, we need to stand tall and raise each other up, rather than mock or judge each other based on what our families have led us to believe.

We have a future as leaders of this planet. It is important you raise your boys to be compassionate and understanding men. Raise your girls to know how important they are, and show them how to be strong.

We are all equally valuable as human beings. Let us care for each other, and not allow any man to teach separation of the sexes.

Remind people it's important to be your authentic selves. Be your truth. Shout it from the rooftops, and when you are told you are too fat, or too dark, or too light, or too short, or just plain not good enough, laugh in the face of that which you know to be a lie.

Be your truth.

I was told so many times that I was not valuable, not good enough, too poor, and didn't fit in. Well, I say, "Fuck it, I'm going to live my story, and maybe one day put it in a book so that those naysayers can read it and know that, against the odds, I made it after all."

I am good enough, and so are you.

I write the way I think, and I walk the way I live.

I am walking the way, and that is why I am free. Establishments or rulers can create walls, but it is up to us to stay behind them or not. If you take anything from these pages, please take the knowledge that you have options. Trust your intuition and if you feel like something isn't right for you, it probably isn't. You have options. Establish what is right and good for you. Remember to do no harm. If you come from a place of gratitude everything will rise up around you. You will find the courage you need to be your authentic self. You can be the light for others on your path to the next thing. Most importantly… Walk your own way and be proud of it.

Acknowledgements

Thank you to my Master Guide for keeping me on my toes with sarcasm and a sense of humor, and to my team for being there when I call on you.

I also want to give thanks to and acknowledge my mentor Sally Baldwin: You have already transitioned, but I still feel you. Thank you for teaching me what you could about channeling, and giving me confirmation after you passed that there is so much more to know.

Janet Nohavec, thank you for your patience and understanding when I attended Arthur Findlay College.

To my mentor Lisa Williams: you fucking rock! You have taught me to remember to trust. Thank you for raising the roof with your energy. It has allowed me to have fun in all of this madness.

Thank you to Ellen Joy Pritchard for her glass bubbles, and for being my friend and Reiki Master Teacher. Thank you for our hike at the vortex in Sedona and for blessing me with the Master Teacher attunement.

Thank you to my spirit brother Paul Samuel Dolman. You hopped on my massage table at the farmers market and kept coming back. You speak my language, and make me feel like I truly belong. Thank you for sharing the Such's, the Hawk, and the espresso.

To the crew at Dos Coffee and Wine in Saint Augustine, Florida, thanks for letting me and so many others squat in the cool vibes long enough to get this down in writing. You are my office. I am grateful for that.

Last but not least, thanks to my best friend Jennifer King for your encouragement, support and for keeping me alive. You only laugh at me when I don't remember which buttons to push on the computer. You don't judge me, and I am grateful for that. You stick with me even though I spew warrior shit. You let me be me and still have me back to sip whiskey on the front porch. Thank you, my soul sister.

www.ingramcontent.com/pod-product-compliance
Lightning Source LLC
Chambersburg PA
CBHW031057080526
44587CB00011B/720